T0365031

MENTAL ALCHEMY

Spiritual Affirmations to Change Your Life

Tabby Sapene, MSW, LISW-S

BALBOA.
PRESS
A DIVISION OF HAY HOUSE

Balboa Press books may be ordered through booksellers or by contacting:

Balboa Press
A Division of Hay House
1663 Liberty Drive
Bloomington, IN 47403
www.balboapress.com
1 (877) 407-4847

Print information available on the last page.

ISBN: 978-1-5043-4143-1 (sc)
ISBN: 978-1-5043-4142-4 (hc)
ISBN: 978-1-5043-4144-8 (e)

Library of Congress Control Number: 2015915562

Balboa Press rev. date: 9/30/2015

I release the old and embrace the new. Abundance, prosperity, and peace fill my soul.

CONTENTS

WITH GRATITUDE

Bella, I am grateful that you have chosen me; my love for you is endless. Carlos, thank you for growing with me on this journey, for your love, patience, and support, and for the gift we share in our daughter.

Thank you to my parents, Christina Piper-Swartz and Pat Suwan, for your love and support.

This book is dedicated to all those who have entered my life in many ways. May you prosper in all ways, as is your Divine Right

To the reader, may these affirmations bless you in all ways possible, for your highest and best good and for the most benevolent outcome.

Many Blessings,
Tabby

INTRODUCTION

What are affirmations? Affirmations are positive words or phrases that one uses to change his or her thoughts and mind-sets. Affirmations for our purposes here include phrases and mantras either spoken aloud, written, or repeated mentally to assist in raising your vibration, changing previous patterns that no longer serve your highest good, and eliciting a deeper way of seeing yourself and the world by mental transmutation.

Mental transmutation is also described as mental alchemy, which is the process of changing and transforming one's own mental states and conditions into more desirable ones.

In ancient teachings, alchemy was described as changing lead into gold. As great teachers, alchemists shared their knowledge with initiates, students in their sacred groups that were cloaked in secrecy for many millennia. These teachings trickled down, bringing esoteric knowledge to all who are ready.

This knowledge brings with it a great capacity for healing and change, as it goes beyond altering the composition of metal and instead focuses on using thought and belief to change one's very mind-set. So the lead (negative thoughts) can be changed into gold (positive thoughts) through the process of mental alchemy. To do so is to change the nature and quality of the very energy around you.

Everything is made up of energy. That energy is ever-changing based on what happens around it, to it, and through it. We emanate our own vibrational energy, which is influenced by the thoughts we think and project out, and by our feelings, emotions, environment, and so on.

As humans, we believe that we have control over many things, and when a desired result to our wishful thinking does not occur, sometimes we become reactive. Usually this results in creating more negative energy because we make an active choice to react in ways that are not beneficial to ourselves or others. Yelling, screaming, or becoming overly emotional do not help change the situation for the better.

There are many things we cannot control, such as the weather or what others will do at any given time or in any situation. The thought that we can control anything is an illusion. However, we have the choice of how we respond to people and events.

Being upset that it's raining isn't going to stop the rain. It's just going to lower our vibrations as we allow ourselves to be in a sour mood. This can happen with whatever we are experiencing if we choose not to change our thoughts about it.

Identifying one's thoughts, feelings, and emotions and addressing these patterns in a healthy way can help one heal in many ways. This in turn can bring one closer to becoming more balanced in mind, body, emotion, and spirit.

One of the reasons we are here on earth is to balance all of our body forms. This brings optimal health and healing on all levels. Our body forms/fields are physical, mental, emotional, spiritual, etheric, astral, and auric. In addition, we have a meridian system and a chakra system.

Since these body fields/forms and systems are extensive, I will only briefly describe each one. The most well-known body field is our physical body. It's the vehicle that our soul picked out to drive for this lifetime. The closest body field to the physical body is the etheric; this extends approximately one quarter to two inches beyond the physical body. This can be seen as a bluish or white/grey color around the body. Kirlian photography can pick up images of this field. The next field is the emotional body. It is fluid in nature as it holds our emotions that are ever changing. Some view this body as blue or grey. From my understanding of this body, the color may change with the emotions that one is experiencing. The emotional body extends approximately one to three inches from the physical body.

The next body the mental body holds our thoughts and mental processes. Extending approximately three to eight inches from the physical body, the mental body may appear as yellow becoming brighter when one is deep in thought or concentrating on mental activities. The color may change to correspond with the emotion(s) that are associated with the thought pattern(s) one has at the time. The astral body is next, extending out approximately one foot from the body. This body form is finer in nature and represents the bridge to the spiritual plane.

The Spiritual body consists of our true nature. Some may describe it as the Higher Self, or what I prefer to call the True Self. This is where we are connected to all that is around us on all levels. In this our nature is that of the Christ Consciousness. This is where we choose to view and treat all souls including ourselves as Divine Spiritual Beings. Despite our many unique differences we are completely equal. No one soul is considered better than another. All of these body forms are contained in the aura or auric body. The aura consists of the seven major chakras, the minor chakras, and the meridian system. The aura can be a multitude of interacting colors and sizes that change depending on the person, their moods, and their physical, mental and emotional health.

Chakras are powerful energy vortexes in your body that interact with the electromagnetic energy field all around you. The earliest known mention of the chakras is in The Vedas the oldest known written tradition in India around 2,500 BCE. In addition, there is information on different models of chakra systems in other traditions including: Tibetan Buddhism, the Jewish Qabalah, Islamic Sufism, Chinese Medicine, and Egyptian Healing.

The basic chakra system includes seven chakras located from the base of your spine to the top of your head. They receive and transmit energy, each one relating to different organs in your body. In addition, each chakra interacts with each aspect of our whole being, physical, mental, emotional and spiritual. When the chakras are open and flowing everything works in harmony.

According to ancient Chinese medicine there are twelve pairs of meridians that are connected to specific organ systems within the human body. When the flow of energy or CH'I to the organs becomes blocked or imbalanced, this may cause dysfunction of the organ system. As noted previously these fields and systems are in constant interaction with one another as they strive to regulate and maintain balance throughout for our ultimate well being.

What we do, say, or think has direct influence over all of our body systems and forms. Quite simply, your body picks up on the messages that it receives from you. These messages have the power and ability to influence the outcome of everything that we experience including illness and disease.

Throughout the years I have read extensively, both scientific journals and those considered alternative or holistic health. I began to see a certain correlation. This seemingly simple thing began to further assist me not only in working with clients for better outcomes in shorter periods of time; it also changed my whole life.

People who are pessimistic about the outcome of a disease or illness that they are experiencing are more likely either to succumb to the disease or have the symptoms for a more prolonged period of time than people who are more optimistic about the outcome.

What does this mean exactly? It means that we have more power than we previously thought over the outcome of what we are experiencing at any given time. The power to heal mentally, physically, emotionally and spiritually first starts with us, not a pill, diagnosis or treatment.

As our body systems and forms interact with one another, they are in constant flow of maintaining balance for our benefit. In reaching a state of balance, we are able to utilize and access abilities that we have long forgotten that we possess. This includes the ability to self-heal. Ultimately we are in charge of our lives. We may not know what the future holds, but we can be in the present moment and control how we respond to any given situation.

An overabundance in one body form, for example, mental, will cause an imbalance in another. Simply put, if you are "all up in your head" all the time, you will not be attuned to what's going on in other aspects of your life. Also, what are we truly missing if we are not living to fully enjoy each moment?

We are not just our minds or bodies. We can see the truth of this as we experience emotions, although how we experience them and interpret them is part of our mental state. Our mental state or thought patterns can be adjusted and changed based on effort, will, and perseverance.

The question to ask would be, "What pattern/thought form do I have that no longer serves me, and what would be a better replacement?"

Example: I cannot _____.

Repeating to yourself that you cannot do something and maintaining that powerful focus actually reinforces the energy around that very thing, allowing it to continue to be something you cannot do.

It is unnecessary to "put out there" that you *can* do something if you're not feeling you can. The focus is not on going from one end of the continuum to the other. However, you could change the thought to

I choose not to _____ at this time.

Therefore you are acknowledging your free will to choose to stay in the same space energetically. When you are ready and feel more confident, you can state:

I am working on _____ for the most benevolent change possible.

This will put you in a state of motion toward your goal. Then you can start to change the phrases or affirmations that you focus on to ones that seem more realistic to you. As you continue to practice daily, you will feel the shift of energy physically, mentally, and emotionally. You will feel the very thing you are working to achieve as if it is already achieved. As you do so, the energetic shift will allow for what you are focused on to change rapidly, in a way that is most beneficial to you.

Imagination is key, as it lends a creative force to the energy that is unlike no other. Visualize yourself doing what you aspire to do; feel the feelings of joy and happiness of actually achieving your goal. Most importantly, allow yourself to experience the difference in you that will take place even before it is completed.

Practice saying this statement: Every day I am becoming better at _____, and I am grateful.

And: I am happy and grateful that I am _____ for the most beneficial outcome!

As you acknowledge that it is your personal choice to change, the energy around the situation, thing, or pattern that you would like to change automatically starts to shift. This shift is due to your newfound openness for something different.

As with anything, steps are required, so be gentle with yourself, keep going, and as you open your mind to possibilities, the results will begin to show and the way will become clearer.

You will find that the suggested affirmations are repeated in multiple sections due to their many uses. You may want to write the affirmations down on index cards or Post-it Notes and place them around your house or keep them nearby, maybe even in your wallet or purse to look at throughout the day. Use the affirmations that resonate with you, and feel free to change the wording as they best suit you.

Blessings and Love,
Tabby

CHAPTER 1

DIVINE LOVE FOR SELF
AND OTHERS

W hat is the concept of Divine Love, anyway? Divine Love is looking at oneself and seeing the perfection that is there. "Perfect? What? Me?" you say as you laugh. Yes, you, with your perceived flaws and all. You know what I'm talking about. You look at yourself and say, "My nose is too big," "I'm not the best communicator," "I am unable to do this or that," or "My life is not how I want it to be." The list can go on and on if you let it. But do you really want to? No, you say with a sigh, almost halfheartedly. I know. I heard you, and I've been there myself.

When we focus on the things we believe are wrong about ourselves, we tend to block out the aspects of ourselves that we need to focus on, those things that make us stand out. And no, I'm not talking about a big nose here. I'm referring to things in us that others will often point out just when we need to see ourselves differently. You know that time when someone a loved one or a stranger commented on something positive about you. Perhaps you blew it off, not wanting to come off as prideful or simply not believing it yourself.

Okay, I see the wheels turning here. As you read this, you can come up with a time or two, perhaps more, when this happened to you. Then, as you smile, to yourself you see the purpose behind that conversation, no matter how short. It was to get you to see yourself differently. To see yourself as you are meant to. You are a Divine Spark of Source Energy, a soul that is very beautiful in every way.

We are so much more than these bodies that we inhabit on earth. We just have forgotten. We have allowed ourselves to believe that we are nothing more than what we do, have, or what we learned from parents, school, society, and others who have influenced us with their own ways of seeing the world.

Although we have learned many positive things from the above-mentioned sources in our lives, we have also learned other things, behaviors, and beliefs that are not always in alignment with who we truly are.

As we identify these beliefs, such as "You can't do that" or "We only do things this way in this family," we see that we can move past these to ones that are a better fit for us.

"Now where does all this fit in regarding Divine Love?" you ask. As we embrace the fact that we are not chained to the past belief systems that we were taught, we can begin to see ourselves and others differently.

That is Divine Love: seeing yourself as you truly are—perfect in every way. Does it happen overnight? No, it takes time and patience. Think about it this way: the belief systems and thoughts you have about yourself took time to form. They did not appear overnight, and they came with a little help from others, right? The most important thing to remember is to be patient with yourself every day, whether you are working at changing how you see yourself or just going about your daily routine.

As you continue on your journey, step by step you will see a new you, one you will be more comfortable with, perhaps one who surpasses all your expectations.

I wish you well on your journey.

Divine Love for Self and Others: Affirmations

❖ I love myself unconditionally.

❖ I radiate universal love.

❖ Everything that comes to me is transmuted to unconditional love and healing.

❖ I infuse myself with unconditional/universal love with acceptance of myself and others where we are on our life path, and I extend forgiveness to all.

❖ Divine Love radiates through me directly from Source toward all others, and I receive back Divine, unconditional love.

❖ I maintain a high vibration full of unconditional love and blessings to all, including to Mother Earth and myself.

❖ Fill my heart with pure love, dear Source. Fill me with forgiveness toward myself and all others. Thank you for allowing me to heal.

❖ Divine Love operating through me blesses myself and others, allowing complete Divine Healing and adjustment to our Divine Life Path.

❖ As I give freely out of love, my abundance flows to me naturally.

❖ Every form of energy that comes to me is transmuted to universal love for myself and toward all others.

❖ Others in my energy field can only enhance and improve my vibrational state.

❖ There is no weakness in love, only strength.

❖ Pure unconditional love surrounds me in every moment, and I open myself up to its transforming abilities.

❖ Divine Love expresses itself through me in all ways for Divine Healing and it is so.

❖ I make my words the vibration of love, release that which is not my true self, and accept who I truly am.

❖ I surrender into what I truly am: pure light. I let go of all negative mental filters and forever feeling the light of love in my heart.

❖ I emanate and express unconditional love in all that I do.

❖ I am a willing receptive, pure vessel of Source for the highest good of all, including myself.

❖ Divine Love prospers us in all ways.

❖ Divine Order and harmony are established in all areas of my life, and I am grateful.

❖ I allow only love in and give out only love.

❖ May all my words and actions be healing to all.

Chapter 2

Forgiveness

R eaching a state of forgiveness comes from our ability to first identify what we choose to forgive. This is not limited to others and their actions; this could also be situations that happened to us in the past, and our own behaviors toward others.

We are very much an active part in the forgiving process because we make the choice whether to open our hearts and minds to forgive or not. And as with so many other things in our lives, forgiveness is just not merely saying words but actually feeling them and allowing a release of the past. Holding on to anger or pain does not hurt the other person or affect the situation the way we may think it does. Holding on to any form of negativity ultimately affects one's own being. This can cause not just emotional issues but health concerns as well.

Studies have shown that some individuals with cancer often have difficulty releasing emotions and hold on to anger and resentment. I found several of these studies from the National Institutes of Health and the Oxford Journals located on their websites. However, there are many more studies from around the world in both scientific journals and alternative health journals that are also easily accessible. I encourage you to explore this on your own.

One could possibly make a correlation that allowing oneself to let strong emotions to fester over time can cause debilitating effects on one's mind and body. Being aware of these effects can enable us to be active participants in our own healing, no matter what situation has occurred, how long ago, and with whom. Even if the other party is no longer in a living body, healing can occur on all levels as we take action steps to take back our own power, not allowing other people or situations to control our lives. This also includes self-forgiveness. I have seen many times in my practice when individuals who have experienced abuse in any form place the blame on themselves.

Healing past pain and forgiving, especially due to trauma and abuse, may take time. As we move forward in life, it's important to honor our feelings, nurture ourselves, and allow the healing to take place in a way we can manage.

Forgiveness: Affirmations

- ❖ I forgive all with an open heart, allowing myself and others to heal.
- ❖ I infuse myself with unconditional/universal love with acceptance of myself and others where we are on our life path, and I extend forgiveness to all.
- ❖ Fill my heart with pure love, dear Source. Fill me with forgiveness toward myself and others. Thank you for allowing me to heal.
- ❖ Divine Love operating through me blesses others, including myself, allowing complete Divine Healing and adjustment to our Divine Life Path.
- ❖ I forgive myself.
- ❖ I release the old and embrace the new. Abundance, prosperity, and peace fill my soul.
- ❖ I allow only love in and give out only love.
- ❖ May all my words and actions be healing to all.

CHAPTER 3

GRATITUDE

With the start of each day, we can actively put in motion for ourselves a day that is focused on joy and gratitude, despite the circumstances around us. We may not be able to predict or control what happens during our day, but we can transmute, lessen, or neutralize negative energy by actively switching our focus onto something more desirable and eventually see the situation that we are in differently. It's all about perception.

How can I choose to see things differently when they are going so wrong? This is a question I have been asked many times and have asked myself numerous times as well in the past. The answer is not through turning a blind eye and ignoring what's going on or pretending the situation is not happening. That does a disservice to you and others who are experiencing difficulty.

The answer is within. We have an innate ability to see things around us—people, places, things, situations—the way we want to see them. Even more specifically, we view them the way we were taught through previous conditioning. As children, we first started identifying with the things around us according to the labels and names that the people in our lives gave those things. Not all of these labels were bad;

however, many were, given due to the labeler's misconception of the person or thing that they were describing.

So is a banana a banana? Well, in English, yes. But in another language it's something else. And we could call it something else entirely if we wanted to. As we do not have one universal language for everyone to adhere to (thank goodness because that would be boring!), so too do we not all see the same things the same way. For one person a banana's good, but for someone who dislikes them, he or she might see bananas as bad.

The coffee you spilled on your shirt the other day was just an inconvenience. A hot, uncomfortable one, but an inconvenience nonetheless, because you had to rush back home and get another shirt. However, for someone else whose day was already riddled with other inconveniences, that person may choose to have a bigger reaction than you did. A few expletives, perhaps? Maybe throwing something? Yet another person who had an even more stressful morning in comparison to the other two might shrug it off and keep heading to work, knowing somehow that the spilled coffee was not that important to the overall scheme of things.

How did they do this, you ask? Willpower. No matter what we experience in our lives, we have the active choice in how we respond to each experience, no matter how debilitating it might seem on the outside. It is how we look at it, our own choice of perception that will define the situation for us.

Is it hard, changing your perspective? Sometimes yes, because we have many ingrained programs that have told us, since birth, how to see the world around us. When we come to a point in our lives were we can identify why we think such things, we say, "Well, because Mom always told me those people always act that way ...," and then we can start to move forward and ask ourselves—really ask ourselves—if those beliefs fit us any longer.

It does take work, but with every step we get closer and closer to a space where we can start living our lives in a state of grace, allowing things that will happen to happen and not elicit an adverse reaction from us.

Are we just talking about spilled coffee here? No, but that's a start. Looking at the little things in life that get under our skin and learning to master those things, not allowing them to get under our skin in the first place, enables us to cope with and successfully handle the bigger things that we encounter in life.

Do you have to choose to see everything as wonderful and beautiful? That's your choice. And it can be a good one if you are in a space where you truly feel that way. However, it may be a simple choice to say to yourself, "I choose not to let that experience affect me in a negative way all day." Or ask yourself, "Did I like it?" Your response may be, "No, but I will focus on whatever else I need to get done today."

It may be simply taking each moment at a time. Stop and have a cup of tea, or take a walk. Get up and stretch. The dishes or paperwork or whatever else that needs to be completed will still be there when you're done.

Usually when we are in the biggest hurry is when our body needs us to take a break. That does not mean shirking our responsibilities but building in moments throughout the day that we honor ourselves by stopping and completely allowing ourselves to enjoy the moment.

Shifting back to gratitude, what are you grateful for? I have a feeling you can come up with things rather quickly when you think about it. Are you grateful for your home, car, food? Even when they might not be what you desire at the moment, they are items that bring you comfort in some way. Expressing gratitude for what you already have brings more abundance in your life, more things for which to be grateful. If you struggle with finding things to be grateful for, just remember you can experience gratitude by simply knowing you have more power over your life experiences than you once thought. You are currently taking action steps to change your life, moving in the direction that will have a more beneficial outcome for you.

Acknowledging you're grateful for what you already have tells the universe that you are ready for more. It allows doors to open that would otherwise be closed. Without a grateful heart we are unable to receive more of what we want and the things that are truly aligned with ourselves.

After we have been through a state of materializing things that we want, we begin to see other things as possibilities. These other things, people, places, and experiences open up a gateway to show us there is much more to life than the things we want. Actually, there are many things that we have not yet considered that may bring us greater enjoyment and fulfillment.

Gratitude: Affirmations

- ❖ I am grateful for this day and my many blessings, which are uncountable.
- ❖ I am grateful for all my blessings and for those unseen.
- ❖ I communicate clearly with the Angels and my Spirit Guides. I am grateful for their guidance, protection, and loving energy and ask Source to bless them continuously.
- ❖ I have faith that all is well.
- ❖ I accept my power to heal myself and others.
- ❖ I am in my full power.
- ❖ My words are powerful. I use them for the good of all others and myself.
- ❖ I am released from any negative beliefs about myself, either self-imposed or from others. I see myself as perfect in the image of Source.
- ❖ I AM strength; I AM love; I AM peace; I AM joy.
- ❖ I focus on the good.

❖ Thank you for my perfect sleep.

❖ Thank you for my perfect health.

❖ Thank you for my perfect breathing.

❖ Thank you for my perfect career in which I am Divinely Guided to utilize my spiritual gifts for the benefit of all.

❖ Thank you for my perfect career, which I have passion in all that I do, and where all my needs are met with surplus.

❖ Thank you for my wonderful, loving, lasting, mutually beneficial, spiritual, sensual relationship with my perfect partner, of which I am so grateful!

❖ Thank you for my caring, responsible friends who are supportive and positive.

❖ I am happy and open to receive everything and everybody that bring increase to my/our greater good!

❖ Divine Love prospers us in all ways.

❖ Thank you that our family is blessed with complete health!

❖ Thank you for unlimited free time to do what I/we desire, which is for my/our greatest good.

❖ Thank you for increased opportunities for spiritual growth.

❖ Thank you for _____ ability to release his or her smoking habit!

❖ Thank you for _____ increased positive decision-making skills that immensely benefits him or her.

❖ Thank you that _____ is led by Divine Intelligence to what benefits their family psychologically, physically, spiritually, and for complete health.

❖ _____ has complete, fully functioning organs, for which I am grateful.

❖ I am grateful that (Name of pet) is potty-trained outdoors, well minded, and chews only on their toys..

❖ Divine Order and harmony are established in all areas of my life, and I am grateful.

❖ How may I serve with balance and abundance?

❖ All that is for my highest good benefit to all, harm to none, including myself comes to me now and in my clear perception of truth I welcome it.

❖ I release the old and embrace the new. Abundance, prosperity, and peace fill my soul.

❖ _____ is completed in Divine Order for the benefit of all.

❖ I ask my Guardian Angels and guides to remove that which isn't for my highest good from all body forms, and I am grateful.

Chapter 4

Knowledge

M any times we as humans see knowledge as the end-all. The more we have in amount and in comparison to others, the better off we believe we are. Or is it so? One can have vast amounts of knowledge stored up but without proper usage of that knowledge, it is meaningless. Meaningless? you ask, but I have to say yes. Without proper application of the knowledge we obtain it is meaningless. For example, if one knows a great deal about a certain subject matter but keeps it to him or herself, that is a personal choice the person makes. If the focus is solely on obtaining more knowledge without sharing it or applying it in his or her life, then all that knowledge is wasted.

Take for example any educational book you have read. You can read it, even memorize it completely, but if you are not applying what you learned, it's not helpful to you. It's just more information stored in the mental vault, and in come cases, our vaults are full of wonderful treasures that are waiting to see the light of day for us and others to fully experience.

That does not mean everything we learn needs to be shared. Also, there are times when others may not be receptive to truly hearing what we have to say. However, there are times when the information we may share may benefit others in some way, even if that means we are planting a seed that will grow over time, allowing them to explore the information when ready. This may also mean stepping out of our comfort zone to share this information. This does not give us free reign to give unsolicited advice whenever we feel like it. What it does mean is following our inner guidance to share something with others who are interested, curious, or simply ask.

A good example may be that you read an article on a natural way for people with type-2 diabetes to lessen their symptoms and maintain balanced insulin levels. You may meet with a friend who comments to you that they want to change their diet and exercise routine to help alleviate symptoms associated with their diagnosis of type-2 diabetes. You can briefly bring up the article and point your friend in that direction. However, if you know someone with that diagnosis, and he or she chooses to do things you believe are harmful to their health, you can choose to share your information with discretion and discernment.

Casually commenting, such as saying, "Hey, I just read an article on decreasing type-2 diabetes symptoms in a natural way. What do you think?" is a good way to see if that person may be receptive to the information you want to share.

Oftentimes when people we care about are going through difficulty, whether with a medical condition, mental-health diagnosis, relationship issues, or something else, we want to jump in and assist. Sometimes we may not see that our "assistance" only pushes others further away, even when we felt we had their best interest in mind.

Allowing others to grow on their journey in their own way is a very freeing thing for them and us. We can be available to share and help when the time is appropriate, and when we use our inner wisdom and not just knowledge, we will be better able to discern when that time is.

Sometimes we can get caught up in being prideful of the subjects we know about, especially if they focus on something that differs from the concerns of the majority. Allowing our ego to come in, we feel a little bit special because of this. Life is not about one-upping anyone in anything. When we choose to see life as such, we miss the true beauty of our differences, we miss out on great chances to share what we know, and we miss gathering new knowledge and experiences from those around us.

With the help of a great teacher, I realized the ego was not something to be feared. The ego is another aspect of us that needs to be healed. So when we feel, see, and know that it's "rearing its ugly head," it is giving us a gift of growth. At this point, our choice could be to identify the pattern(s), let the pattern(s) continue, or take active steps to heal that aspect of us that is ready to be healed.

Ego can go both ways. It can influence us to do, say, or think too much or too little. Let's look at my experience. Someone pointed out to me (multiple times, mind you), as he pointed to his head and to me, that I had all this knowledge and quite frankly, I wasn't putting it to good use. At the time I understood his words, but I wasn't yet receptive to implementing anything. I had been in the helping profession for some time but took a break for family reasons, and even though I wanted to return to work, I was hesitant.

I was having a "Piglet" moment. The image of Piglet (from *Winnie the Pooh*) shaking and saying, 'Oh da-da-da-dear ..." comes to mind. I was in the process of going through profound personal healing and for many reasons wasn't ready to come out of my shell.

Over time and after much personal healing, I came to the point where I asked myself a very important question. This question alone would be a strong catalyst for change, propelling me forward like a catapult. "What good was all the information and skills that I learned if I was not sharing them with others?"

It was just stored up, unused, unapplied for the most part. Useless. My intuition had been guiding me to share what I knew with others. And most certainly there were times when ego came up, giving me very easy, convenient excuses not to. After going within and seeing that what I had learned in knowledge and skills could be helpful in some way, I knew I needed to move forward. There came a point in my life where there was no other choice.

I came to a clear realization of what I knew before and had tried to talk myself out of. I had identified part of my Divine Soul Purpose: to use the knowledge and skills that I gathered and continue to do so to assist others on their life path. It can be as simple as sharing a short insight if asked that might assist someone at the time. Other times it is over mental-health and energy-therapy sessions to assist in whatever way is most beneficial.

I, like everyone else, have been caught up in getting by, doing what needs to be done, living day-to-day in this cycle. Life is so much more than that. I had a taste of it as I worked from the comments I received from clients, seeing people come from a state of despair not wanting to go on and then completely changing their lives around.

The gratitude I received in a comment from a parent of a client a long time ago is a great example. After about a year of intensive therapy, the client was being discharged. After the family and I finished the last session, the mom came up to me and said, "Thank you for giving me my daughter back."

In moments like these, I am reminded that things that seem so mundane in our lives, the things that seem routine, may have the most meaning and growth of all. To me I was doing my job, but to that family I was doing a lot more.

With gaining the knowledge (or remembering) that everything is energy, I was able to recognize the ripple effect that all we do has many lasting effects on everybody and everything around us.

All knowledge, no matter how great or small we perceive it to be, can be applied to help others and ourselves through this journey that we decided to take. And yes, you did decide to be here at this time. You chose to come at a pivotal time, a time of transition on earth for your soul's purpose.

Knowledge: Affirmations

❖ My knowledge comes clearly and directly from Divine Intelligence Source.

❖ I completely understand and utilize Divine universal laws for the highest good of all.

❖ I have the power to change.

❖ I have the power to control how I view my experience.

❖ I affirm that I am the only one who has power over my mind, body and spirit.

❖ I have the power to control my train of thought.

❖ I release all negative emotions from my subconscious.

❖ I am in the present moment.

❖ I free myself from limited patterns of thinking.

❖ I am in control of my life as I release negative patterns quickly and easily, moving into a higher state of consciousness.

❖ I allow my highest good to come to me this day and in my clear perception of truth I welcome it.

❖ I am in my full power.

❖ I release all belief systems that do not serve my highest good.

❖ My words are powerful; I use them for the good of all others and myself.

❖ I am released from any negative beliefs about myself, either self-imposed or from others. I see myself as perfect in the image of Source.

❖ I AM strength; I AM love; I AM peace; I AM joy.

❖ I focus on the good.

❖ Thank you for my perfect spiritual, abundant career in which I utilize my gifts fully for others and myself.

❖ I allow Divine Balance in all areas of my life.

❖ I am aligned with my higher self. I am connected and fully utilize Divine Substance for our greater good.

❖ Divine Order and harmony are established in all areas of my life, and I am grateful.

❖ How may I serve with balance and abundance?

❖ All that is for my highest good, benefit to all harm to none, including myself, comes to me now, and in my clear perception of truth I welcome it.

❖ I release the old and embrace the new. Abundance, prosperity, and peace fill my soul.

CHAPTER 5

SPIRITUAL/INTUITIVE ABILITIES

I can feel eyebrows rise as people look at this. Many questions and comments are coming up now. I don't have any abilities. What is intuition? For those who are not familiar with this topic, I will give a brief overview.

Number-one thing for you to know: *everyone is intuitive.* Each of us is born with our own set of abilities meant to assist us on our journey here.

You know the feeling you get when you are getting close to someone or about to do something and it does not seem right? Some may describe it as bad vibes. That person does not seem trustworthy, so you back away. You have a feeling to turn down a different street because the one you usually take looks backed up with traffic.

When we acknowledge these feelings and take steps to listen to them when we have them, we will continue to open up, which will increase our intuition.

Not all intuitive feelings are about negative things. You may get the feeling to call someone at a particular time, and at that time that person was thinking about you and wanted to connect with you. Ever been at the right place at the right time? You know, where everything was just working out? You met someone who was helpful in some way, or found something you needed.

This is part of using your intuition. Of course your Spirit Guides and Angels are there assisting you to make sure you are where you need to be at the right time. This is especially true when something important is about to happen in regard to your soul purpose. Our guiding influences are very important to us while we are on this journey. They will be discussed at length in their own chapter.

Back to abilities: there are numerous to talk about. I will briefly describe the ones that are most commonly known.

Clairsentience is the ability to clearly feel. With this ability you can feel what's going on around you. You may feel people's moods before they even interact with you. You may feel energy forms around you such as Spirit Guides, Angels, and deceased loved ones. You may also even feel the pain of others. For example, in the energy therapy work that I do, I can feel when someone might a have pain in a certain area, such as his or her back. This ability helps me in that it guides me to work directly on that area to assist in alleviating the pain.

With clairsentience, as with other abilities, it is important not to fear them as you experience them. Sometimes when your abilities are opening up, you may not understand what's happening and possibly interpret them in a way that makes you more fearful.

That said, some things may seem a little spooky at first. I know I've had my moments earlier on in life where I let fear take over, making things much worse than they needed to be.

Fear, as with any other negative emotion, lowers one's vibration and actually brings more of those types of experiences. When in doubt of what you are experiencing, you can always ask your Spirit Guides and Angels for clarification and assistance.

If you are feeling an abrupt change in mood, it is likely that you are picking up on the emotions of others. Just stop and ask yourself whether it is your true feeling. In most cases, you will get a clear feeling if it is yours. If it isn't, you can affirm out loud or in your mind, "This is not my truth. I release it to be healed, and I am attuned to my own true feelings."

Clairvoyance is clear seeing. This is not limited to seeing things, objects, and spirits with your own naked eye right in front of you. This can also mean seeing things in your mind's eye. For example, you may be thinking about what to buy your friend for her birthday, and as you are deep in thought, a picture of a book pops into your mind. You may buy the book or get a gift card to a bookstore. The friend may reply that she had been thinking about and wanting to buy that book for a while.

Loved ones may also wish to communicate with you in this fashion. You might not be able to see Grandma Rose pop up next to you as you're cooking dinner, but you may get pictures of roses in your mind that remind you of her.

Clairaudience is clear hearing. Like clairsentience, this can happen in multiple ways. You may hear a voice call your name out loud and look around for the source. Or you could hear something in your mind like, "Don't forget the milk," as you are about to leave the grocery store. Not everything you hear will be profound and life changing. There are those around who are helping you by making your life a little easier with this communication. So you go back into the grocery store, buy the milk, and say a thank you out loud or in your head, whatever you are more comfortable with. It is important to acknowledge your helpers, as they are with you to assist you during this lifetime. You of course have free will, so the choice is yours.

Claircognizance is clear knowing. This is when you have information about something that you know is correct but are unsure how you know it. You may overhear a conversation and chime in with the information needed. Or you may ask yourself something and the answer is provided.

Wrapping up on abilities for now, I want to make one major distinction. There is a difference between a psychic and a medium. A psychic is someone who can read your energy field and the thought forms in it. This includes thought forms from the present lifetime and past ones. Not all are skilled at understanding where the thought form originates. It could even be a projection from someone else's thoughts about you. Psychics give you information based on what they interpret from your auric field (aura).

A medium is able to communicate with those in spirit and get information. This may include but is not limited to Spirit Guides, Angels, and deceased loved ones.

If you choose to get information from either a psychic or a medium, keep in mind that not all information you receive may be 100 percent accurate. Some things can be lost in translation. Sometimes the messages we might receive, whether getting information for others or ourselves, may be altered by our misperception.

Not all psychics or mediums are spiritually inclined. Therefore, keep in mind they may not have your best interest in heart. They, just like other people, are more than happy to get payment for services rendered. True *Divine Guidance* is different. Information that is given to you for your highest and best good from your Spirit Guides and Guardian Angels will be put in a way that does not scare you or separate you from others.

An example would be someone giving you a message saying it looks like you are getting a divorce. This would lead your thoughts and energy down that path even if you were only having issues with your spouse that could be worked on if you both chose to do so. From my own spiritual understanding, those who give messages in such a way will reap what they sow. No one, no matter what title, has the right to interfere with your free-will choices or soul purposes. All the relationships we are in have specific purposes for our own soul growth.

Returning to the message that you received, the message to you instead might be that your Spirit Guides are assisting you with your relationship and are asking you both to look at how you are communicating with one another. Please remember that if the information that you receive does not feel right, just let it go. Trust your own inner compass, your own intuition.

If you choose to be involved with any psychic, metaphysical, energy healing, or spiritual group, be mindful of how these groups feel to you. Do you feel good when you leave these groups? Do you feel drained when you leave? Do you feel supported? Does something feel off to you? Do they request you do things that do not resonate with you? This not only applies to these groups but to all other groups and people as well. Remember to explore your feelings because they are valid, and they may hold the key to more information that you might not have been aware of before.

Please keep in mind that your abilities may differ from others', and you may not express them through the ways previously discussed. In addition, your abilities will develop in a way that is for your highest and best good. Having an intuitive ability open up completely without proper guidance and support may not be the best solution for you. Keep in mind all will happen in Divine Right Timing. This may mean letting go of fear in regard to your abilities and removing or healing blocks associated with your abilities from this lifetime or previous ones. Therapeutic past-life regression may assist with this. Vibrational/energy therapy focusing on the chakra system can do so as well. The terms vibrational therapy, energy medicine, and vibrational medicine are used interchangeably. They are based on the scientific principles that all matter vibrates to a precise frequency. By using specific vibrations, balance can be restored to matter that is unbalanced.

The terms energy therapy, energy healing, spiritual healing, and sometimes energy medicine are also used interchangeably. These are branches of alternative medicine where healers channel energy,

(CH'I, Ki, Prana, etc) into a patient. Knowledge of these therapies has been passed down through many ancient texts associated with different cultural traditions from India, Egypt, China and Japan among others. Some vibrational/energy therapies include; reiki, acupuncture/acupressure, crystal/stone therapy, light/color therapy, sound/music therapy, and EFT.

It has been my personal experience from my own journey that someone with intuitive abilities with a clinical background may be more effective and better able to bring a more balanced approach to healing on all levels. However, this depends on the person, his or her approach, skill level, life experiences, and other factors. Delivery is also important. It's often not what you say but how you say it that can greatly affect how one takes the information given. Remember the earlier example regarding the message about divorce?

There are others who, like me, have a clinical background and are highly intuitive. For many reasons, others may be unwilling to publicly express this part of themselves, mostly, I believe, due to the possibility of ostracism. I too had debated about moving forward in not only writing this book but also in expanding my private practice, opening a wellness center to address the spiritual aspect of our lives that effect us immensely. In many cases, we do not fully understand this aspect of ourselves, and in others there are not many support systems out there, including mental-health professionals who are willing or able to assist us on this part of our journey. And with good reason. Many mental-health professionals are in positions where they are grossly underpaid, undervalued, and experience burn out from long hours with clients with a myriad of different needs. Then you add productivity ... but I digress.

All in all, many professionals are not sufficiently trained in this area, and many are reluctant to explore it despite their own abilities because they may believe the outcome may not end up in their favor due to others' misconceptions and fears. And what do people fear most? What they don't fully understand!

By reading others' work, such as Dr. Wayne Dyer, Dr. Brian Weiss, Louise Hay, Dr. Judith Orloff, Doreen Virtue, Catherine Ponder, and others, and seeing their personal and spiritual growth through their writings has immeasurably helped me release my own fear of moving forward into my own soul purpose. I thank those authors for their inspiration, which has ultimately propelled me forward on my journey.

Spiritual/Intuitive Abilities: Affirmations

❖ I am intuitive.

❖ I use my abilities for the highest and best good of all.

❖ I am a powerful and accurate medium for others and myself (if this is something you choose to work on and is part of your soul purpose).

❖ I am powerfully and accurately clairvoyant (clear seeing) (if this is something you choose to work on and is part of your soul purpose).

❖ I am powerfully and accurately clairaudient (clear hearing) (if this is something you choose to work on and is part of your soul purpose).

❖ I am powerfully and accurately clairsentient (clear feeling) (if this is something you choose to work on and is part of your soul purpose).

❖ I am powerfully and accurately claircognizant (clear knowing) (if this is something you choose to work on and is part of your soul purpose).

❖ I am attuned to my own true feelings.

❖ I am grateful for my Guardian Angels and, Spirit Guides, and I am open and receptive to their guidance.

❖ I communicate clearly with the Angels and my Spirit Guides. I am grateful for their guidance, protection, and loving energy. And I ask Source to bless them continuously.

- ❖ I allow my abundance to flow to me endlessly.
- ❖ I allow/accept Divine Guidance from Source, my Higher Self, Archangels, Angels, and Spirit Guides.
- ❖ Pure unconditional love surrounds me in every moment, and I open myself up to its transforming abilities.
- ❖ I have the power to change.
- ❖ I have the power to control how I view my experiences.
- ❖ I affirm that I am the only one who has power over my mind, body, and spirit.
- ❖ I have the power to control my train of thought.
- ❖ I am in my full power.
- ❖ I release all belief systems that do not serve my highest good.
- ❖ My words are powerful. I use them for the good of all others and myself.
- ❖ I am released from any negative beliefs about myself either self-imposed or from others. I see myself as perfect in the image of Source.
- ❖ I AM strength; I AM love; I AM peace; I AM joy.
- ❖ I focus on the good.
- ❖ Thank you for my perfect spiritual, abundant career in which I utilize my gifts fully for others and myself.
- ❖ I allow Divine Balance in all areas of my life.
- ❖ I emanate and express unconditional love in all that I do.
- ❖ I am a willing receptive, pure vessel of Source for the highest good of all including myself.
- ❖ I love myself unconditionally.
- ❖ I am mentally, physically, emotionally, and spiritually balanced.
- ❖ Divine Love prospers us in all ways.
- ❖ I am aligned with my Higher Self. I am connected and fully utilize Divine Substance for our greater good.
- ❖ Thank you for increased opportunities for spiritual growth.

❖ Thank you for constant positive focus, which increases my spiritual and personal growth.

❖ I release all that is not for my highest good in my life, work, and relationships. Divine Order is established, allowing my greatest good in!

❖ How may I serve with balance and abundance?

❖ All that is for my highest good, benefit to all, harm to none including myself comes to me now, and in my clear perception of truth I welcome it.

❖ I release the old and embrace the new. Abundance, prosperity, and peace fill my soul.

❖ I am attuned to nature.

❖ I am in clear contact with my Spirit Guides and Guardian Angels, those beings that are for my highest and best good, only and I am grateful.

❖ I am Divine Source Energy.

❖ I remember my dreams and completely understand them.

❖ I am precognitive (if this is something you choose to work on and is part of your soul purpose).

❖ I ask my Guardian Angels and Spirit Guides to remove that which isn't for my highest good from all body forms, and I am grateful.

CHAPTER 6

ABUNDANCE

A bundance and prosperity can take many forms. What we generally think of first is money or objects that we desire. These are not bad things in contrary; they are an important part of our lives. There is a misconception among some religious and spiritual groups that state money is not good. Money is nether bad nor good. It is a form of currency that sometimes can be used for positive or negative reasons, just like our mind power.

Other forms of abundance are all around us. These can come in the form of ideas, opportunities, creative endeavors, etc, as I touched on in the gratitude section, and which is worth repeating now.

Acknowledging that you are grateful for what you already have tells the universe that you are ready for more. It allows doors to open that would otherwise be closed. Without a grateful heart, we are unable to receive more of what we want and the things that are truly aligned with ourselves.

Think about it this way. If you are constantly doing things for someone else and this person appears aloof and ungrateful to all you are doing, do you think you will choose to continue that particular pattern? In some cases, people will continue doing so due to lack of boundaries, being codependent, or an inability to see the pattern, etc.

However, there is a point when most people come to the realization that enough is enough.

But what if that person is grateful for all that you do? How do you generally feel about that? As you feel that person's gratitude many times, it will fuel you to give and do more with a grateful heart. Well, the universe does the same, projecting more energy into what we need, want, or desire as in accordance with natural laws, and what is in alignment with our highest good or true self.

After we have been through a state of manifesting things we want, we begin to see other things as possibilities. These other things, people, places, and experiences open up a gateway to show us that there is much more to life than the things we want. Actually, there are many things we have not yet considered that may bring us greater enjoyment and fulfillment.

What are these things? you may ask. They are everything, because the universe is limitless. You are limitless potential. You have the ability to create a life of happiness for yourself just by using your free-will choices to be happy, content and grateful, even when the circumstances may appear otherwise.

You are limitless potential. What are you going to create today?

Abundance: Affirmations

- ❖ I allow my greatest good to flow to me endlessly.
- ❖ Blessed with Divine Knowledge, I go forth into this day allowing Divine Guidance to guide me, bring me/lead me to my highest good.
- ❖ I bless others and am grateful for their abundance as I radiate and allow my abundance to come into my life.
- ❖ As I give freely out of love, my abundance flows to me naturally.
- ❖ I allow my highest good to come to me this day, and in my clear perception of truth I welcome it.

- ❖ I am in my full power.
- ❖ I release all belief systems that do not serve my highest good.
- ❖ My words are powerful. I use them for the good of all others and myself.
- ❖ I am released from any negative beliefs about myself, either self-imposed or from others. I see myself as perfect in the image of Source.
- ❖ I AM strength; I AM love; I AM peace; I AM joy.
- ❖ I focus on the good.
- ❖ Thank you for my perfect spiritual, abundant career in which I fully utilize my gifts for myself and others.
- ❖ I allow Divine Balance in all areas of my life.
- ❖ Thank you for my perfect career in which I am Divinely Guided to utilize my spiritual abilities for the benefit of all.
- ❖ Thank you for my perfect career, which I have passion in all that I do, and where all my needs are met with surplus.
- ❖ I emanate and express unconditional love in all that I do.
- ❖ I am mentally, physically, emotionally, and spiritually balanced.
- ❖ Divine Love prospers us in all ways.
- ❖ I am aligned with my higher self. I am connected and fully utilize Divine Substance for our greater good.
- ❖ Thank you that all we have is paid in full with surplus to our family.
- ❖ Thank you that our family is blessed with complete health!
- ❖ Thank you for unlimited free time to do what I/we desire, which is for my/our greatest good.
- ❖ Thank you for increased opportunities for spiritual growth.
- ❖ This project is funded completely in all areas!
- ❖ Divine Guidance has led me to the perfect office for my business!
- ❖ Thank you for constant positive focus, which increases my spiritual and personal growth.
- ❖ I have completed _____ successfully!
- ❖ Thank you for increased positive family interactions.

❖ Thank you for our many relaxing, enjoyable family vacations!

❖ Thank you for Divine Restoration and surplus of all our accounts!

❖ I release all that is not for my highest good in my life, work, and relationships. Divine Order is established, allowing my greatest good in!

❖ Divine Order and harmony are established in all areas of my life, and I am grateful.

❖ How may I serve with balance and abundance?

❖ All that is for my highest good benefit to all, harm to none including myself comes to me now, and in my clear perception of truth I welcome it.

❖ I release the old and embrace the new. Abundance, prosperity, and peace fill my soul.

❖ _____ is completed in Divine Order for the benefit of all.

CHAPTER 7

HEALING

W hat is healing? Healing is something that can occur on many levels of being. Healing can be the change of energy in any body form that is not in harmony with perfect well-being to a higher level of energy that is more harmonious. Healing may not be the same as a cure, although with healing, a cure can be manifested.

For example, a person with a degenerative disease such as cancer may receive a complete cure, left with no traces of the disease. Their body may be cured, but they might not have addressed the cause(s) of their illness. Another person with the same disease may receive healing that allows him or her to identify the root causes of the illness, which the person may choose to acknowledge and move forward from, regardless of whether he or she is completely cured.

As they address their illnesses and come to terms with them, people are able to heal on so many levels. Their bodies may not be cured, but their spirits are able to identify with the impact the illness has on them and on those around them.

This allows for a greater spiritual understanding of one's life, prompting the person to ask questions such as, "What truly is my life purpose?" and "What have I done or am I doing to fulfill it?"

These questions may come up at any time in our lives without being prompted by an illness. Sometimes great change can elicit these questions. However, all self-exploration facilitates a desire for healing oneself.

As we heal certain aspects of our lives, we can see other parts of us open up to healing, facilitating a domino effect. Healing can be spontaneous, or it can take time. The process of healing will happen in a way that we can handle.

Let's look at addressing healing on all levels. Any illness—mental, physical, emotional, and spiritual—that occurs in any of our body forms may not have had an origin in this lifetime. We see this in past-life regressions, where a patient may have symptoms that there may be no clinical or medical explanation for at present. For example, they may have pain in their arm with no history of an injury at that site. And they may have extensive tests done that come up with no medical or clinical diagnosis. During a past-life regression, they might have an experience in which they see themselves wounded at that very site of the pain in a different century in a different country.

As you move forward in your life I encourage you to continue any medical care that you are receiving that has been helpful to you, and to seek alternative methods of healing that can be incorporated into your health care regimen.

Healing: Affirmations

❖ My chakras are clear, clean, and aligned and radiate Divine Healing Energy, which is infused and emanates in and around my auric field.

❖ Divine Love operating through me blesses others, including myself, allowing complete Divine Healing and adjustment to our Divine Life Path.

❖ Divine Balance activates all of my chakras and meridians to produce a clear connection to my higher self.

❖ Pure unconditional love surrounds me in every moment, and I open myself up to its transforming abilities.

❖ I have the power to change.

❖ I have the power to control how I view my experience.

❖ I affirm that I am the only one who has power over my mind, body, and spirit.

❖ I have the power to control my train of thought.

❖ Divine Love expresses itself through me in all ways for Divine Healing and it is so.

❖ I make my words the vibration of love, release that which is not my true self, and accept who I truly am.

❖ I surrender into what I truly am: pure light. I let go of all negative mental filters and forever feeling the light of love in my heart.

❖ I release all negative emotions from my subconscious.

❖ I am in the present moment (this is where you focus on the here and now, releasing concerns about the past and worries about the future. These keep you from truly experiencing this present moment.)

❖ I free myself from limited patterns of thinking.

❖ I am in control of my life as I release negative patterns quickly and easily and move into a higher state of consciousness.

❖ I allow my highest good to come to me this day, and in my clear perception of truth I welcome it.

❖ I have faith that all is well.

❖ I accept my power to heal others and myself.

❖ I am in my full power.

❖ I release all belief systems that do not serve my highest good.

❖ My words are powerful. I use them for the good of all others and myself.

- ❖ I am released from any negative beliefs about myself, either self-imposed or from others. I see myself as perfect in the image of Source.
- ❖ I AM strength; I AM love; I AM peace; I AM joy.
- ❖ I focus on the good.
- ❖ Thank you for my perfect spiritual, abundant career in which I utilize my gifts fully for others and myself.
- ❖ I allow Divine Balance in all areas of my life.
- ❖ I emanate and express unconditional love in all that I do.
- ❖ I am a willing, receptive, pure vessel of Source for the highest good of all including myself.
- ❖ I love myself unconditionally.
- ❖ Thank you for my perfect sleep.
- ❖ Thank you for my perfect heath.
- ❖ Thank you for my perfect breathing.
- ❖ I am mentally, physically, emotionally, and spiritually balanced.
- ❖ Thank you that our family is blessed with complete health!
- ❖ Thank you for unlimited free time to do what I/we desire, which is for our greatest good.
- ❖ Thank you for increased opportunities for spiritual growth.
- ❖ Thank you for _____ ability to release his or her smoking habit!
- ❖ Thank you for _____ increased positive decision-making skills that immensely benefit him or her.
- ❖ Thank you that _____ is led by Divine Intelligence to whatever benefits their family psychologically, physically, and spiritually and for complete health.
- ❖ _____ has complete, fully functioning organs, for which I am grateful.
- ❖ Divine Order and harmony are established in all areas of my life, and I am grateful.
- ❖ How may I serve with balance and abundance?

❖ All that is for my highest good, benefit to all, harm to none including myself comes to me now, and in my clear perception of truth I welcome it.

❖ I release the old and embrace the new. Abundance, prosperity, and peace fill my soul.

❖ I allow only love in and give out only love.

❖ I ask my Guardian Angels and Guides to remove that which isn't for my highest good from all body forms, and I am grateful.

CHAPTER 8

STRENGTH

H as anyone ever told you that you have great inner strength? You
do. You might question it, but the fact that you chose to be here
and learn and grow from many soul lessons is proof of that.

What if you were told that you have been here before, on this
earth, and perhaps other places as well? How does that make you feel?
Something you want to think about? These are questions for you to
ponder, and I'm not here to convince you.

What I do know is that every experience you have had in your life
has led you to where you are today. As you look back, I'm sure you
or others who have observed your life could point out things that you
have done, accomplished, and/or grew from.

Looking back on what you have already lived through can be a great
catalyst for growth as you acknowledge your Divine Inner Strength and
move forward through whatever it is that troubles you at the present
moment.

Sometimes when we are in the middle of something painful, it
is hard to see past that pain to what lies ahead. And there are times
where we just want to say uncle and give up. It's at this time where we
may reach a point and ask, "What is the meaning of this experience?"

When we reach that point, we allow Divine Healing in. Being receptive to understanding the meaning of what we experience in life can allow us to alter our viewpoint of our experiences enough to let in another stream of energy. That may mean seeing the situation as it truly is, something that has brought us to rock bottom to get us to change. Hard as it may be, that change can be a step toward something greater, something that we previously could not imagine in the mindset we were in. This change may take time.

In the meantime, we can utilize affirmations and other techniques to assist us on our journey and to remind us that we have great inner strength, more than we can ever imagine.

Strength: Affirmations

* ❖ Divine Love prospers all and unites, giving us Divine Guidance and strength.
* ❖ I have the power to change.
* ❖ I have the power to control how I view my experience.
* ❖ I affirm that I am the only one who has power over my mind, body, and spirit.
* ❖ I have the power to control my train of thought.
* ❖ I have faith that all is well.
* ❖ I accept my power to heal others and myself.
* ❖ I allow/accept Divine Guidance from Source, my Higher Self, Angels, and Spirit Guides.
* ❖ I am in my full power.
* ❖ I release all belief systems that do not serve my highest good.
* ❖ My words are powerful. I use them for the good of all others and myself.
* ❖ I am released from any negative beliefs about myself, either self-imposed or from others. I see myself as perfect in the image of Source.

- ❖ I AM strength; I AM love; I AM peace; I AM joy.
- ❖ I focus on the good.
- ❖ Thank you for my perfect spiritual, abundant career in which I utilize my gifts fully for others and myself.
- ❖ I allow Divine Balance in all areas of my life.
- ❖ How may I serve with balance and abundance?
- ❖ All that is for my highest good, benefit to all, harm to none including myself, comes to me now, and in my clear perception of truth I welcome it.
- ❖ I release the old and embrace the new. Abundance, prosperity, and peace fill my soul.
- ❖ I allow only love in and give out only love.
- ❖ _____ is completed in Divine Order for the benefit of all.
- ❖ I ask my Guardian Angels and Guides to remove that which isn't for my highest good from all body forms, and I am grateful.

CHAPTER 9

BLESSING OTHERS

What you give out comes back in all forms. Many times we are fixated on ourselves. "I want this." "How will this work out in my favor?" "I won't do this *because* it makes me feel this way." As the ego takes, over we see everything and how it affects us individually.

I am not suggesting we do not address things that may affect us in a negative fashion, but to take a step back and see how the things in our world affect not just us but others as well.

We are all connected; we all come from the same creator: Divine Source Energy, God, Infinite Intelligence—whatever you would like to call them, if you so choose to at all.

Acknowledging that you came from the same loving energy source as your neighbor, the mailman, the elected official you just read about, and everyone else is a big part of one's journey.

Seeing others with they eyes of love, unconditional love, allows us to flow Divine Energy out to them, which in turn comes back to us. Simply put, as we bless others, we receive blessings back.

Are there times we don't feel like blessing others because they are behaving in a way that we don't appreciate? Yes. But remember that we can make the choice. We choose what we think, remember! Most importantly, *we choose* how we respond to others. We can choose to see them as separate from ourselves and only see them as the behavior they are expressing at that time.

Do you recall a time when you had a less-than-stellar moment? Perhaps you decided to take your frustrations out on a loved one or whomever you came into contact with at that moment. How did you feel after that? If you say not so good, you can probably also identify that you wouldn't want to be treated that way yourself.

Here's an experiment. Whenever you are feeling down about anything or anyone, I want you to stop for a moment and think about it differently.

Does that person have financial issues? Health concerns? Something else that might concern him or her? Identify something you believe this person might be looking to change in his or her life for the better; don't dwell on it for a long period of time. Briefly acknowledge it and imagine that person with the issue resolved. Does he or she look happy? Healthy? Is he or she doing things differently?

Visualize them how you think this person would look and continue to see him or her as such if the issue crosses your mind. You can also do this exercise for yourself, picturing yourself a certain way, and feeling the feelings that you want to feel in order to assist with changing your energy field, train of thought, and raising your vibration to another level.

There is a disclaimer to this. There are people who are going through soul lessons by experiencing illnesses and other issues. This might not be their time to fix or heal the concern until they learn their soul lesson. For example, take someone who is always rushing around nonstop. Then suddenly he or she falls and breaks a leg. Now this person has to take the time to stop, heal, and see if this is how he or she wants to continue living, by rushing from one thing to the next.

If this person chooses to push what they physically can do before being completely healed, it will take longer for healing to occur. In this case, you can still picture this person the way he or she would look as completely healed.

One simple and easy way of blessing others that I use on a daily basis is sending what I call "blessings and (unconditional) love". You can do this while driving and passing others by, or when walking by others in the grocery store. Just look in their direction, smile at them (whether or not you catch their attention) and state "blessings and love" to yourself. You don't need to have a specific outcome in mind. Simply doing it with the intention that whatever is most benevolent for that individual will happen is sufficient enough. You can also use this technique when thinking about others.

In the end, blessing others not only helps them but us as well. As we bless others, we take our minds off ourselves, allowing us to be helpful to others, and when done with an open, loving heart, it feels good.

Blessing Others: Affirmations

❖ I bless others and am grateful for their abundance as I radiate and allow my abundance to come into my life.

❖ My house/home/office is blessed by Divine Source and the Angels, allowing all who dwell here to unite in love, have Divine Rest and fulfilling relationships.

❖ As I give freely out of love, my abundance flows to me naturally.

❖ I communicate clearly with the Angels and my Spirit Guides. I am grateful for their guidance, protection, and loving energy. I ask Source to bless them continuously.

❖ Thank you for my wonderful family/friends/coworkers, who are filled with unconditional love, guided by Angels, and Spirit Guides, whom I have harmonious relationships with.

❖ Divine Love expresses itself through me in all ways for Divine Healing and it is so.

❖ I make my words the vibration of love, release that which is not my true self, and accept who I truly am.

- ❖ I surrender into what I truly am: pure light. I let go of all negative mental filters and forever feeling the light of love in my heart.
- ❖ Thank you for my perfect spiritual, abundant career in which I utilize my gifts fully for others and myself.
- ❖ I emanate and express unconditional love in all that I do.
- ❖ Divine Love prospers us in all ways.
- ❖ Thank you that our family is blessed with complete health!
- ❖ Thank you for unlimited free time to do what I/we desire, which is for our greatest good.
- ❖ Thank you for _____ ability to release his or her smoking habit!
- ❖ Thank you for _____ increased positive decision-making skills that benefits him or her immensely.
- ❖ Thank you that _____ is led by Divine Intelligence to what benefits his or her family psychologically, physically, and spiritually and for complete health.
- ❖ _____ has complete, fully functioning organs, for which I am grateful.
- ❖ (Name of pet) is potty-trained outdoors, well minded, and chews only on their toys.
- ❖ How may I serve with balance and abundance?
- ❖ All that is for your highest good, benefit to all, harm to none including yourself comes to you now, and in your clear perception of truth you welcome it.
- ❖ I release the old and embrace the new. Abundance, prosperity, and peace fill my soul.
- ❖ I allow only love in and give out only love.
- ❖ May all my words and actions be healing to all.
- ❖ I ask _____ Guardian Angels and Guides to remove that which isn't for their highest good from all body forms, and I am grateful.

CHAPTER 10

DIVINE RELATIONSHIPS

What are Divine Relationships? The first and most important Divine Relationship that you will ever have is with yourself. We are all part of Source Energy/Infinite Intelligence, and we are all connected. To simply say treat others, as you would want to be treated is not enough. First we must ask ourselves, "How do I truly want to be treated?" because we have forgotten or simply do not know how we want to be treated. We have observed over the years what we think is the norm of how to treat others and how we *should* expect others to treat us.

However, as we look back at our lives and these examples, we can identify behaviors that we do not wish to continue receiving from others or to give out ourselves.

As we identify these behaviors and acknowledge that we would like them to change, we can move forward by visualizing how we would like to be treated. Do you want to feel more accepted in your relationships? Look at how you are interacting with others. Are you able to accept others even though they might not be acting in a way that you believe is acceptable? The answer is not to condone their behaviors but to start to see them how you would like them to be.

An example would be arguing with a loved one. If you have been arguing frequently and there appears to be no resolution to the disagreement, you may want to change the flow of energy by changing your expectations of the outcome.

Here's a scenario. You are on your way home from work and begin to get a queasy feeling in the pit of your stomach. You think, *Oh, I really don't want to see Ralph because we will start to argue over finances again.*

As that thought and feeling starts, you can mentally say to yourself: *STOP.* Then replace the image of going home and seeing Ralph. For the first time in a week, you pause, look at him, and say, "How was your day?" You can visualize what you think he would say. Now remember, if it does not seem realistic to you, do not picture that image. So if you have been fighting for more than a week, your partner may not great you with a warm hug and suddenly everything is happily ever after.

However, if that is your goal, you can visualize that and be aware that that particular outcome may not happen on the first day. Visualizations are very powerful, especially when we back them up with positive energy. If you are very angry and are having trouble coming out of that emotion, first you need to do some self-care to get yourself to a point where you can see someone or something in a different light. This may mean taking a time out or break. Take a walk, read a book, or do some meditation or breathing techniques discussed in the chapter on meditation and grounding.

In addition, as much as possible, focus on what your ideal intended outcome is unwaveringly. If you think about the positive outcome but then start to ruminate on the things that went wrong before, you are breaking the positive stream of energy and essentially living in the past. That is not where you want to be in order to move forward into a different outcome.

Back to Divine Relationships. I could discuss kindred souls, souls mates, twin flames, and other relationships that we choose to have while we are here on earth. For now, the most important thing to know about all relationships is that they are all valid; they are all a means for us to grow.

How are we to move on in our lives and build strong relationships if we are not willing to take the time to put forth the effort to allow these relationships to grow? In turn, are we willing to see when we are at a point in our soul growth that we now recognize when we are ready to let a relationship go? Are we willing to learn the lessons that came with the relationship, ones that will help us build stronger relationships?

To love others unconditionally, we must choose to love ourselves first. Allow yourself to fall in love with the uniqueness that is you. You are a Divine Being, a Divine Spark of Source Energy. Identify those qualities you can bring to a relationship, and be willing to work on what no longer serves you. Who knows what kind of love you will experience?

Divine Relationships: Affirmations

❖ My house/home/office is blessed by Divine Source and the Angels allowing all who dwell here to unite in love, and have Divine Rest and fulfilling relationships.

❖ As I give freely out of love, my abundance flows to me naturally.

❖ Thank you for my wonderful family/friends/coworkers, who are filled with unconditional love, guided by Angels, and Spirit Guides, whom I have harmonious relationships with.

❖ Every form of energy that comes to me is transmuted to universal love for myself and toward all others.

❖ Others in my energy field can only enhance and improve my vibrational state.

❖ There is no weakness in love, only strength.

❖ Divine Love expresses itself through me in all ways for Divine Healing, and it is so.

❖ I make my words the vibration of love, release that which is not my true self, and accept who I truly am.

❖ I surrender into what I truly am: pure light. I let go of all negative mental filters and forever feeling the light of love in my heart.

❖ I allow my abundance to flow to me endlessly.

❖ I allow/accept Divine Guidance from Source, my Higher Self, Angels, and Spirit Guides.

❖ Thank you for my wonderful, loving, lasting, mutually beneficial, spiritual, sensual relationship with my perfect partner, of which I am so grateful!

❖ Thank you for my caring, responsible friends who are supportive and positive.

❖ I am happy and open to receive everything and everybody that bring increase to my/our greater good!

❖ I emanate and express unconditional love in all that I do.

❖ Divine Love prospers us in all ways.

❖ Thank you that our family is blessed with complete health!

❖ Thank you for unlimited free time to do what I/we desire, which is for our greatest good.

❖ Thank you for increased opportunities for spiritual growth with _____.

❖ Thank you for _____ ability to release his or her smoking habit!

❖ Thank you for _____ increased positive decision-making skills that benefits him or her immensely.

❖ Thank you that _____ is led by Divine Intelligence to what benefits his or her family psychologically, physically, and spiritually and for complete health.

❖ _____ has complete, fully functioning organs, for which I am grateful.

❖ (Name of pet) is potty-trained outdoors, well minded, and chews only on their toys.

❖ Thank you for increased positive family interactions.

❖ Thank you for our many relaxing, enjoyable family vacations!

❖ Thank you for Divine Restoration and surplus of all our accounts!

❖ I release all that is not for my highest good in my life, work, and relationships, and Divine Order is established, allowing my greatest good in!

❖ Divine Order and harmony are established in all areas of my life, and I am grateful.

❖ How may I serve with balance and abundance?

❖ All that is for my highest good, benefit to all, harm to none including myself comes to me now, and in my clear perception of truth I welcome it.

❖ All that is for our highest good, benefit to all, harm to none including ourselves comes to us now and in our clear perception of truth we welcome it.

❖ I release the old and embrace the new. Abundance, prosperity, and peace fill my soul.

❖ I allow only love in and give out only love.

❖ _____ is completed in Divine Order for the benefit of all.

❖ May all my words and actions be healing to all.

❖ I ask _____ Guardian Angels and Guides to remove that which isn't for his or her highest good from all body forms, and I am grateful.

CHAPTER 11

DIVINE CAREER

o you love what you do? Does it make you feel fulfilled at the
end of the day? Do you feel you are Divinely Guided to do what
you currently do? Have you asked yourself these questions?

If not, that's okay, but maybe now is the time. This does not mean
you have to quit what you are doing this minute and sit in meditation
until you get the answer of what your Divine Career is. There are some
people who have done that, and it has worked for them. However, for
the rest of us, first we have to be aware of and open to change to get
our lives on track with what our hearts desire in a vocation.

Any change can be frightening at first —at least that's what the
ego would like us to believe. Often, altering the way we look at
things, especially change, can make the transition easier, sometimes
effortless. When we see ourselves in a state that we no longer wish to
be in, for example a job that is unrewarding and unfulfilling, we can
acknowledge those thoughts and feelings and start to identify what we
truly want to do.

Here is an exercise. Take a notepad and draw a line down the
middle, making two columns. On the top of the left side write
Current Job Pros and on the top of the right side write **Current
Job Cons**. Now, without judging or thinking too long, on each side

write down the first thing that comes, uncensored and unedited, to mind. You may find that as you write something on one side, something will pop into your head to write on the other side. Feel free to go back and forth as needed.

Now look at your paper. Is one side fuller than the other? Read what you wrote. Is there anything you wish to add? Do so until you feel you are finished. As you look at the pros, did you put that you are compensated in some way? It might not be how or in the amount you would like, but you still are. Is that the main reason why you are at this job? If so, I want you to write down little things that you might not have thought about before that make your life/day easier at that job (such as my coworker is always helpful, or my commute is only ten minutes). You can put these positives on an index card (the same with affirmations), and you can pull them out and look at them whenever you need a reminder to shift your focus at work.

If you start to put your focus and attention on these little things while you are working instead of what you do not enjoy, you will find that your day will get easier and easier.

You can also use your notepad to write down reflections you have throughout the day or when you get home. Also, write down your frustrations. Then rewrite them in a way that you would have preferred the situation had gone. Focus only briefly on what happened that you did not like and then close your eyes and visualize the same thing with a different ending, one that is most beneficial and benevolent to all.

For example, the conversation you had with your boss that left you feeling drained and frustrated now ends with you clearly stating why something happened. Do so in a direct, nonconfrontational way, asking for clarification if needed. You visualize yourself being open to talking through the situation without becoming aloof or going to the other extreme and becoming reactive.

As you have started to work on this mind—set, releasing that which is undesirable, you can bring your focus on what you would like to see different in your work. Ready for an entire overhaul? Ready to move into something different? Now you are ready to look at what is your Divine Purpose.

Divine Career: Affirmations

❖ My house/home/office is blessed by Divine Source and the Angels, allowing all who dwell here to unite in love, and have Divine Rest, and fulfilling relationships.

❖ Thank you for my wonderful family/friends/coworkers, who are filled with unconditional love, guided by Angels, and Spirit Guides, whom I have harmonious relationships with.

❖ Every form of energy that comes to me is transmuted to universal love for myself and toward all others.

❖ Others in my energy field can only enhance and improve my vibrational state.

❖ There is no weakness in love, only strength.

❖ Divine Love expresses itself through me in all ways for Divine Healing and it is so.

❖ I make my words the vibration of love, release that which is not my true self, and accept who I truly am.

❖ I surrender into what I truly am: pure light. I let go of all negative mental filters and forever feeling the light of love in my heart.

❖ I allow my abundance to flow to me endlessly.

❖ I allow/accept Divine Guidance from Source, my Higher Self, Archangels, Angels, and Spirit Guides.

❖ Thank you for my perfect spiritual, abundant career in which I utilize my gifts fully for others and myself.

❖ I allow Divine Balance in all areas of my life.

❖ Thank you for my perfect career, in which I am Divinely Guided to utilize my spiritual abilities for the benefit of all.

❖ Thank you for my perfect career, in which I have passion in all that I do, and where all my needs are met with surplus.

❖ I emanate and express unconditional love in all that I do.

❖ Divine Love prospers us in all ways.

❖ This project is funded completely in all areas!

❖ Divine Guidance has led me to the perfect office for my business!

❖ Thank you for constant positive focus, which increases my spiritual and personal growth.

❖ I have completed _____ successfully!

❖ I release all that is not for my highest good in my life, work, relationships, and Divine Order is established allowing my greatest good in!

❖ Divine Order and harmony are established in all areas of my life, and I am grateful.

❖ How may I serve with balance and abundance?

❖ All that is for my highest good, benefit to all, harm to none including myself comes to me now, and in my clear perception of truth I welcome it.

❖ I release the old and embrace the new. Abundance, prosperity, and peace fill my soul.

❖ _____ is completed in Divine Order for the benefit of all.

❖ May all my words and actions be healing to all.

CHAPTER 12

SOUL PURPOSE/LIFE MISSION

E very soul has a purpose. Actually, souls have many, not just for themselves but for others they contracted with throughout each lifetime. We contract into this human existence mainly to grow spiritually and move up as souls to a higher level. This may take many lifetimes through each soul lesson and purpose until we have completed each one and move on to another.

Many times soul growth can be rapid, when we choose multiple lessons at one time and are able to identify and learn these lessons. For those things that we struggle with on a continuous basis it can be of great benefit that we look at these things and ask ourselves, what is the purpose of this? What is this person, thing, or situation teaching me? As we look at what we go through as soul lessons and gifts of soul growth, they allow us to see the bigger picture, the deeper meaning of what appears to be struggles, hardship, and pain.

What is the calling of your heart? Have you ever had that feeling or longing to do something that drives you to better yourself in a way that nothing else does? If not, that's okay. Let me ask you this. Have you had any desire to do something that may better yourself in some way? Something you are drawn to that you feel may be enjoyable?

If you have ever had these feelings and put them off, you're not alone. It is all too easy to get caught up in the cycle of day-to-day life and tend to put things off that we desire to do. It may be due to finances, time, or our own fears that we do this. In doing so, we cut off apart of ourselves that needs to have these experiences to live, grow, and enjoy life.

Acknowledging the things we want to do or experience in life leads us to finding the time, money, and ability to do them, even if it is only what some would call the little things, like taking a walk outside or having a cup of tea. When we do things unhurried and allow ourselves to experience all that is around us at the time, our awareness starts to become more expansive.

Smell the hot drink in front of you. Taste the crisp tartness of the apple. Feel the softness of the grass beneath your feel. Listen to the water as it rushes down the stream. Let your eyes delight in the beauty that is around you.

Becoming more aware of everything allows us to be in the stream of Divine Consciousness, which connects us with everything and everyone, including our Higher Selves and our Divine Purpose.

As we move forward with each incarnation, each growth, we are more attuned to what this purpose is. We may see ourselves in a dream, a vision, in another lifetime doing the same thing. We may get reminders from the universe at different stages of our life, calling us to wake up and move forward into what we agreed to do.

This does not mean that we do the same thing in each lifetime; we do have free will to make the choice to do something different in each one. However, the knowledge that we attain over our lifetimes is forever with us, even if we are not accessing it directly all of the time.

Chances are you have thought about your purpose before, or you may even know what it is for you. Some people, despite much prompting by signs, feelings, etc., disregard them because they are not yet ready to address them fully. That's okay; it's important to remember that everything happens in Divine Right Timing, even when ego may tell us otherwise.

If you are receiving information, test it in your mind or out loud: "Is this for my highest and best good, and for the highest and best good of others as well?" "Is the information that I received benevolent?" Trust your intuition, and move forward with faith. You can ask your Higher Self, Guardian Angels, and Spirit Guides for clarification.

You may even get the feeling that you are on your chosen path, but you may need to stay there and wait patiently and allow the next step to happen, or you need to move ahead, and the action steps you need to take will be given to you.

You can ask for all the help that you need from Universal Source, and it will be there. It may not appear in the way that you think it should, but it will come. Most important is putting out into the universe that you are ready for the next step and allowing the guidance to come. Remember to put out positive energy/thoughts about what you would like to do even if you do not know exactly what that is yet. It is not your job to know what or how exactly but to be in a state of allowing.

Sometimes the help will come in ideas that may bring you closer to what you want. It may be in the form of clear action steps that come, or you may meet someone who gives you a suggestion. You may pick up on something that is useful in a conversation that you overhear, or see something on a sign as you walk by. There are no limits on how Divine Intelligence will work. Energy is limitless and so are you, so don't put restrictions or limitations on your good by saying or thinking it *has* to come in a certain way at a certain time.

The signs will be there. However, this is your life, and you have free will to choose. You may also have to do things like take action steps, sometimes when you may not feel like doing them.

Assess the situation and ask yourself if what you need to do will be helpful and if there is any reason why you should not do it. Then ask yourself if the reasons for not doing them include any aversion to change and/or being unwilling to put forth the effort. You may even have some fears in regard to going past your comfort zone into the unknown and relinquishing trying to control the situation. Thanks okay too, acknowledge how you feel about the situation. That's the first step to move forward. Then you can make your choice.

Back to soul purpose. Go with your gut, take one step at a time, and remember that we are not only here for ourselves but for others as well. There are many souls who are here to help you fulfill your Divine Purpose. Some will assist you in a time of need by giving guidance, or assistance in some way. Others will teach you a life lesson, such as in our personal relationships. You can choose whether or not you will let these lessons break you or help you grow.

Remember, you have the power to control your actions, responses and deeds. That does not mean that we do not experience sadness, sorrow, anger, frustration, and a whole myriad of emotions throughout our existence. However, we have the choice to identify, acknowledge, and express them appropriately. We can also allow ourselves to release and clear past repressed emotions in our energetic fields and allow ourselves to heal.

In truth, we are always here for each other. To learn, to grow, and to move forward no matter what our specific soul purposes are. And as part of our journey, we can lend a helping hand along the way to others who may benefit from our compassion, kindness, knowledge, or time. In doing so, our lives and the lives of others will be enriched.

Soul Purpose/Life Mission: Affirmations

❖ I am fully aware and accept my soul's goals, and I am open to Divine Guidance, which is assisting me on my journey.
❖ I completely understand and utilize Divine Universal Laws for the highest good of all.

❖ As I release past patterns/choices, they are replaced with new ones that fit my soul's goals.

❖ Divine Balance activates all of my chakras and meridians to produce a clear connection to my higher self.

❖ I communicate clearly with the Angels and my Spirit Guides. I am grateful for their guidance, protection, and loving energy and ask Source to bless them continuously.

❖ Thank you for my wonderful family/friends/coworkers who are filled with unconditional love and guided by Angels and Spirit Guides, whom I have harmonious relationships with.

❖ I have the power to change.

❖ I have the power to control how I view my experience.

❖ I affirm that I am the only one who has power over my mind, body, and spirit.

❖ I have the power to control my train of thought.

❖ I release all negative emotions from my subconscious.

❖ I am in the present moment.

❖ I free myself from limited patterns of thinking.

❖ I am in control of my life as I release negative patterns quickly and easily and move into a higher state of consciousness.

❖ I allow my highest good to come to me this day, and in my clear perception of truth I welcome it.

❖ I am in my full power.

❖ I release all belief systems that do not serve my highest good.

❖ My words are powerful. I use them for the good of all others and myself.

❖ I am released from any negative beliefs about myself, either self-imposed or from others. I see myself as perfect in the image of Source.

❖ I AM strength; I AM love; I AM peace; I AM joy.

❖ I focus on the good.

❖ Thank you for my perfect spiritual, abundant career in which I utilize my gifts fully for others and myself.

❖ I allow Divine Balance in all areas of my life.

❖ Thank you for my perfect career in which I am Divinely Guided to utilize my spiritual gifts for the benefit of all.

❖ Thank you for my perfect career, in which I have passion in all that I do, and where all my needs are met with surplus.

❖ Thank you for my wonderful, loving, lasting, mutually beneficial, spiritual, sensual relationship with my perfect partner, of which I am so grateful!

❖ Thank you for my caring, responsible friends who are supportive and positive.

❖ I am happy and open to receive everything and everybody that bring increase to my/our greater good!

❖ Divine Order and harmony are established in all areas of my life, and I am grateful.

❖ I emanate and express unconditional love in all that I do.

❖ I am mentally, physically, emotionally, and spiritually balanced.

❖ I forgive myself.

❖ Divine Love prospers us in all ways.

❖ I am aligned with my Higher Self. I am connected and fully utilize Divine Substance for our greater good.

❖ Thank you for unlimited free time to do what I/we desire, which is for our greatest good.

❖ Thank you for increased opportunities for spiritual growth.

❖ This project is funded completely in all areas!

❖ Divine Guidance has led me to the perfect office for my business!

❖ Thank you for constant positive focus, which increases my spiritual and personal growth.

❖ I have completed _____ successfully!

❖ How may I serve with balance and abundance?

❖ All that is for my highest good, benefit to all, harm to none including myself comes to me now, and in my clear perception of truth I welcome it.

❖ I release the old and embrace the new. Abundance, prosperity, and peace fill my soul.

❖ I allow only love in and give out only love.

❖ _____ is completed in Divine Order for the benefit of all.

❖ May all my words and actions be healing to all.

❖ I ask my Guardian Angels and Guides to remove that which isn't for my highest good from all body forms, and I am grateful.

CHAPTER 13

ARCHANGELS, ANGELS, GUARDIAN ANGELS, AND SPIRIT GUIDES

H ave you felt a comforting presence during a time of need? Did something fall into place for you in your life with little effort for you, just the desire that it would happen? These instances and many others can be accounted for by your spirit team, which some call your spirit band.

There are times when loved ones visit you, comfort you with their presence, and assist in some ways. However, they are not always around us 24/7. They have jobs to do in the spirit world, just as we do when we are there, and they have other loved ones to visit.

Some may believe that our loved ones/family members are there to guide us, and in some ways they may. But we must use discretion and discernment from whom we receive any guidance, whether in flesh or spirit.

Besides, do you really want financial-planning assistance from your grandma if she could not even balance her own checkbook? All kidding aside, those who are here to guide us on many different levels have training to do so in specific areas. And there are beings that who do not. Being open and receptive to Divine Guidance is good, but being open to anything is not.

I have had conversations with people who stated they wanted to be open to anything. I asked, "Do you really want to be open to anything?" I understood that once someone becomes aware of certain spiritual aspects of life, they want to take it all in, to learn all they can in the search for answers and truth. However, we must temper our enthusiasm with discernment.

After they think about it for a moment, the implications set in. After all, we were not just talking about being open to change. From my experiences and interactions, I believe there are beings who are here for benevolent purposes. But there are others just like us that have free will choice.

Do we all have others' best interest in heart when we make choices? I venture to say no, not all the time. And in some cases, due to the level of soul development and choice, some do not consider their connection with others and the impact their decisions have, especially when those decisions may be adverse.

We have the ability to surround ourselves with loving beings who can assist us. Also based on our vibrational level, the energy that we put out we can be open to lower vibrational beings. If one chooses to be angry all the time and intentionally harm others, he or she emits a certain energy pattern. Whereas someone who is heart-centered in their decision-making, being compassionate, even-tempered, and calm in responding is going to emit a different, energy pattern.

When we choose this energy of unconditional love despite what circumstances around us dictate, we operate on a higher vibration. Higher vibration does not imply "better" in a sense that the person is better than others who make different choices. In most cases, it means the energy is clearer, more balanced, with heartfelt intent, and for those who are clairsentient, it feels better. Remember back to a time when you were in a foul mood. How did that feel? Not so good, right?

Now remember a time when you were laid back, not rushing, and felt like you were in the flow. Did you feel better then? Of course! That is an example of you vibrating energetically at two different levels.

You can also feel this or have a feeling about the different energy levels when you are interacting with others. You may feel someone's sadness or grief at a funeral or their elation at a birth.

As with people, you may experience this with animals, nature, and inanimate objects because they all have their own energetic fields, just like us. Yes, the table you got at the garage sale has a certain vibrational energy too. You may have been drawn to it because it held energy of many great comforting family meals that took place on it over its lifetime. Just like having a keepsake from a deceased family member, we may feel a connection to its loving memories or an aversion to it if the person was pessimistic all of the time.

Going back to energetic beings that may not have your best interests in mind. They may be drawn to lower-level energy that you emit. What this means is if you are dabbling in the occult using Ouija boards and other things that are not attuned to a high vibrational loving energy, you may have contact with beings that emanate at that frequency. Essentially, what you are doing when you use a Ouija board is saying, "Hey, I want to contact the dead. I want information, and I don't care where its source is from." And many times there will be something there willing to make contact with you—and it won't always be benevolent.

If you do feel or sense energy around that you are unable to explain, please do not feel fearful. That may be your first response, but it will not be helpful. Lower-level energies/entities feed off of your fear. In fact, they may do things to try to make you fearful, frustrated, or angry because they know that then you will not be operating at your best vibration.

When we are at a lower vibration and ungrounded, we tend to not make the best decisions for ourselves. This is because we are not our true selves, Divine Beings who emanate energy that can be most loving and healing for ourselves and those around us. See the following chapter on how to become grounded.

Try to distinguish what form of energy is around you if you can. If not, that's okay. You may ask for Divine Intervention from those beings that are benevolent and loving to you. It can be as simple as stating in your mind that you would like assistance *only* from your Spirit Protector or Guardian Angel who is a part of your personal truth. These beings can and will help when asked but will not go against your free will choice; they feel loving and kind and will not give you any information that will make you fearful.

If you do not understand what type of energy is around you, you do not have to interact with it. Chances are when it sees that it can't affect you by making you react in a fearful or angry way, it will lose interest.

It is important that even if we can get assistance from the spirit world that we focus on our own claircognizance, clear knowing, and follow our own intuition. We are not here to give our lives over to any being in order to make our decisions for us. We are here to have experiences, learn, and grow. We are here to live from our own higher selves, from our own soul to develop our own intuition, which is our true connection to Divine Universal Source.

While I am writing this, I am receiving guidance that assists me when I feel stuck, sometimes bringing me information that helps me move forward. As I do energy therapy on others in my practice, there are beings that specifically guide me with that. For all the guidance and assistance that I receive, I am very grateful.

There are many ways to "get in touch" with those beings around you who care for you, some of which include acknowledging signs that you see around you. These signs will be presented in such a way to get your attention, to help you, but are sent in a manner that will not frighten you.

I have had multiple clients state that they saw a "form" starting to materialize in front of them but then they reacted by yelling or becoming fearful, very quickly that being faded away in all cases because it did not want to frighten the person. Some discussions with clients ended up in a good laugh as they realized they just shrieked at Aunt Mildred, who just wanted to say hi.

Loved ones who come back to visit do so to express love or give information. Messages like "I'm okay," "I'm not in pain anymore," "I love you," or "I put the will in the curio in the basement" are often shared.

In some cases, spirits may need help. They might not know or understand that they left their body. In such cases, explaining to them that they passed and to go toward the light, where they will be with other loved ones, may help. They have free will too, so they can decide to stay and hang out at the old farmstead because it's "theirs." Usually when we physically die our soul leaves, and we naturally gravitate to the light where others are waiting for us.

Receiving Divine Assistance. I personally have had money manifested during a time of need. I felt the urge to go out and walk after a deep snow. It was cold and windy. I was walking on top of a snow bank, and there was no evidence anyone besides myself had tread on the freshly fallen snow. As I looked down there was a twenty dollar bill, which looked clean and new. I was overcome with gratitude and joy because I was then able to go and buy much-needed food for my family. Also, when I went to the store I was able to use coupons for exactly what I needed, which helped even more!

In these instances, we can choose to play them off as coincidences. I could have told myself that someone dropped the money, although there were no other footprints. I could have stated that the wind blew it up there, but what were the odds that it was there at exactly the time I was there? And remember, I followed my intuition to go outside at that time; my ego mind did not want any part of going out! I have been helped in other ways throughout the years, for which I am grateful. This was only one example.

Can you think of any in your own life? As you think of those times in the past where you were Divinely Assisted, you can still say thank you, quietly or out loud, and those who helped will be delighted that you recognized their assistance. As you acknowledge this more and more, signs will be open to you in a way that you can handle them. So don't be afraid that your Spirit Guides will jump in front of you and say hi. They know what you are ready for.

To personally meet your guides, all you have to do is ask. They will not do anything that would scare you. I have assisted clients in identifying their primary Guardian Angels, Spirit Protectors who are assigned to come with us before we choose as souls to enter our body for this lifetime. Their main purpose is to keep us in our body so we complete our purpose and guide us on our life path.

What do you mean by keeping me in my body? you may ask. Have you ever misplaced your keys to find them in the same spot later on? Have you ever been late to a meeting because of traffic? Maybe these were sources of frustration to you. What if you found out that in both cases there was an accident, which you could have been part of had you not been stopped by these things happening? Slipped on a stair but did not fall down all the way? Felt something cautioning you from doing something that you wanted to do really badly and then found out later what the consequences could have been if you had followed through?

These are some of the ways that Divine Benevolent Beings intervene. Now, we do have free will, and they will not violate that even when they want to help us. So if you're getting the feeling that you might not want to have another drink but you do it anyway, that is a free-will choice.

Now there are times in our lives and in the lives of others where one has a major accident, illness, or death, which is all part of the plan the person involved has signed up for. In any case, neither Angels nor Guides will interfere, but they will help the soul through it.

What I want to be clear about is that we have signed up for certain things for our spiritual growth and the growth of others that we are interacting with.

Remember our previous example where a person who is extremely overactive to the point of exhaustion may develop an illness or have an accident where he or she breaks a leg, causing that person to stop and reevaluate his or her life? This may lead to a change in direction that they might otherwise not have considered before because they did not allow the time to do so. No matter what happens, even when it feels like it is too much, we have those around us who can and will help. All we have to do is ask, and be open to the guidance we receive.

Another way to meet your Spirit Guide and Angels is through meditation, which I will discuss in the next chapter.

Archangels are celestial beings that transcend time and space and can assist us. Do not worry that you are taking away time from someone else who might be in more dire conditions than yourself if you call on them. Archangels can be with many people at once. They only need to be called upon.

Archangels have been linked to many different religious and spiritual groups over many lifetimes. Their names have different spellings, and they are described slightly different based on the beliefs of the individual and group. Angelic beings are mentioned in the following ancient texts: the Hebrew Bible, Christian Bible, Qur'an, Hadith, Talmud, Essenes, Apocrypha, and the Qabalah, to name a few.

Here I will give a very brief description of some belief systems and their description of angelic beings.

Hinduism is one of the world's oldest living religions. We have scriptures that date back nearly six thousand years for Hinduism. Besides the major Gods, there are a host of minor Gods called *devas* (feminine form is called *devi*). The word deva means shining one. They were believed to inhabit the astral plane, the higher plane of existence. Devas played the role of protector to humans. It was believed that, though spiritual in nature, devas could appear to us in human form and were believed to bring messages or help guide people in their spirituality.

In Zoroastrianism, the ancient religion that developed in Persia around 1,000 BCE, it is believed that a being referred to as a *Fravashi*, a Spirit Guardian, was with each individual. These were beings of light that manifested the energy of the Divine. It is believed that each person has at least one Fravashi.

The Jewish scriptures use the term messenger of God to refer to Angels. Angels are mentioned in the Talmud and Qabalah. Angels were seen as semi-divine beings who were never human, who served God, and who were not to be idolized. Angels were given the tasks to bring messages, sometimes to help people, sometimes to test them.

In Ancient Greece, Aristotle believed in the "first mover," an immortal being who never changed, who was responsible for the order and wholeness of the universe. He also believed that as there was a first mover, there must be "second movers." In neo-Platonism, the second movers became associated with Angels. The word Angel actually comes from the Greek word *angelos*.

Many sects of Christianity have accepted angelic beliefs from Jewish scriptures that have been passed down since before Christ. The New Testament also includes more references to Angels. Angels were the ones who told of the coming of Christ. In the gospels, it's an Angel who appears to Mary to tell her she's with child, and an Angel appears to Joseph to tell him Jesus will be God's son. It's also angels who appear to the shepherds in the fields to announce the birth of Christ.

Islam shares some tenets with both Judaism and Christianity, however it has its own traditions and teachings concerning Angels. Angels are mentioned repeatedly in both the Qur'an and the Hadith. Islam teaches that angels are God's messengers. They are intermediaries between God and humanity. Unlike humans, they have not been given the gift of free will. Their job is to act as messengers and serve as guardians, encouraging mankind to do good, countering the temptations placed before humanity. It is part of the six articles of faith in Islam to accept Angels.

In the Baha'i faith, Angels are seen to come to us as confirmations that there is a celestial, powerful God and to reveal God's "abounding grace" to humankind. They're described as blessed beings that have severed the attachment to this earthly world.

This is just a short synopsis of Angels in various religions. This information is not intended to represent all members of any specific faith, nor does it represent the full rich history of any belief system. Currently, many people who consider themselves nonreligious, spiritual, agnostic, or even atheist continue to believe in the presence and intervention of Angels in human life.

Just like us all, Angels and Spirit Guides have specific purposes for their being. I have included some information on different Angelic beings in the following affirmations. There are many Angels in existence, and I have included information on some who are more well known. However, there are many more.

If you wish to call upon Angels and forget their names, just put the intention out there, and the right one will come. For example, say, "Angel who helps with relationships, can you please help me heal this relationship between me and my son for the most benevolent outcome of all?"

There are different guiding influences that we have over our lifetimes that do not continuously remain with us. As we are learning about a subject or skill or going through a specific issue in our life, we may acquire a different guiding influence. And if we choose to not utilize a certain skill set further due to free will, those guiding influences may move on to others who need assistance.

All Angels and Spirit Guides come to you out of unconditional love. They will give you information to assist you in healing yourself mentally, physically, emotionally, and spiritually and for continuing on your life path. There is nothing you can do or have done in the past that would break that bond of love that your Spirit Guides and Guardian Angels have for you. Remember that always.

Archangels, Angels, Guardian Angels, and Spirit Guides: Affirmations

❖ My house/home/office is blessed by Divine Source and the Angels, allowing all who dwell here to unite in love and have Divine Rest and fulfilling relationships.

❖ Thank you for my wonderful family/friends/coworkers, who are filled with unconditional love, guided by Angels and Spirit Guides, with whom I have harmonious relationships with.

❖ I allow/accept Divine Guidance from Source, my Higher Self, Angels, and Spirit Guides.

❖ I clearly identify and communicate with my Spirit Guides and Guardian Angels, those beings for my highest and best good only, and I am grateful.

❖ I give my Spirit Guides and Guardian Angels permission to intervene in helpful ways to assist me in my life's journey.

❖ I give my Spirit Guides and Guardian Angels permission to intervene and assist me to make healthy choices in my life.

❖ I give my Spirit Guides and Guardian Angels permission to intervene for my highest and best good to keep me focused on my soul purpose(s).

❖ I am grateful for my Spirit Guides and Guardian Angels who are guiding me every day.

❖ Archangel Michael surrounds me and clears away all lower vibrations, and I am grateful.

- ❖ Thank you, Archangel Michael, for guiding me through my Divine Life Purpose. I am grateful.
- ❖ Thank you, Archangel Michael, for reminding me of who I truly am, a Divine Soul, and I move forward now in my Divine Soul Purpose in strength and in peace.
- ❖ Archangel Ariel surrounds me with strength and courage, and I am grateful.
- ❖ Archangel Ariel fills me with abundance in mind, body, and spirit.
- ❖ Archangel Raguel, please assist me in maintaining Divine Balance and order in my life; I am grateful.
- ❖ Archangel Raguel, thank you for helping me distinguish my clairsentient feelings. I know which are my own and which are others'.
- ❖ Archangel Raguel, please assist us in resolving this situation in a way that is fair and just to all involved.
- ❖ Archangel Uriel, thank you for helping me know what to do to move forward in my life. I am grateful.
- ❖ Archangel Uriel, thank you for helping me connect with Divine Wisdom. I am grateful.
- ❖ Archangel Gabriel helps me strengthen my leadership skills so I may help and lead others, and I am grateful.
- ❖ Thank you, Archangel Gabriel, for assisting me in using my creative abilities of self-expression in loving ways. Thank you that, as I do so, I am helping heal others and myself.
- ❖ Archangel Jophiel helps me to see the beauty all around me, and I am grateful.
- ❖ Archangel Jophiel, thank you for helping me find time to enjoy nature.
- ❖ Archangel Jophiel, thank you for helping me clear away everything that no longer serves me from my physical environment.
- ❖ Archangel Jophiel, thank you for helping me become patient with myself and others. I allow everything in my life to unfold in benevolent timing.

❖ Thank you, Archangel Raphael, for assisting me in connecting and maintaining Divine Relationships.

❖ Archangel Raphael guides me as I heal others and myself, and I am grateful.

❖ Thank you, Archangel Raphael, for guiding me in ways to heal myself naturally.

❖ Archangel Raziel helps me remember Divine Esoteric Knowledge from Source that I utilize to assist others and myself for spiritual growth, and I am grateful.

❖ Archangel Raziel, thank you for helping me increase my clairvoyance and see the beauty of Divine Source all around me.

❖ Archangel Chamuel guides me to my Divine Career on this life path, and I am grateful.

❖ Thank you, Archangel Chamuel, for helping me heal my relationships.

❖ Thank you, Archangel Chamuel, for helping me manifest Divine Loving Relationships.

❖ Thank you, Archangel Chamuel, for helping me to see that only love is real; my soul is filled with peace.

❖ Archangel Zadkiel, thank you for giving me clarification through clairaudient signs that I receive, and I am grateful.

❖ Archangel Zadkiel, thank you for helping me forgive myself and others, seeing all with the eyes of compassion.

❖ Thank you, Archangel Zadkiel, for assisting me in increasing and maintaining my memory functioning.

❖ Thank you, Archangel Zadkiel, for increasing my knowledge and helping me in teaching others about what I know to assist them in their spiritual and personal growth.

❖ Thank you, Archangel Azrael, for comforting me in my time of grief.

❖ Thank you, Archangel Azrael, for helping my loved ones in their time of grief/transition. Please help me use words that heal in this situation.

❖ Thank you, Archangel Sandalphon, for assisting me in recognizing and receiving the Divine Answers to my prayers!

❖ Thank you, Archangel Sandalphon, for helping me appreciate all the miracles that happen in my life.

❖ Thank you, Archangel Metatron, for guiding me in ways to assist children in developing their spiritual gifts and remembering who they truly are.

❖ Archangel Metatron, thank you for using sacred geometry to clear, clean, and align my energy centers.

❖ Archangel Metatron, thank you for guiding me to prioritize and organize my life, allowing me to live more efficiently and fully.

❖ Thank you, Archangel Jeremiel, for assisting me in a life review. Please give me the courage to release past patterns that no longer serve my highest and best good.

❖ Archangel Jeremiel, thank you for guiding me to be merciful and compassionate in this situation, for others and myself.

❖ Thank you, Archangel Haniel, for your nurturing, healing energy.

❖ Thank you, Archangel Haniel, for guiding me in increasing passion in all areas of my life.

❖ Thank you, Archangel Haniel, for allowing me to identify and trust my intuitive abilities.

CHAPTER 14

MEDITATION AND GROUNDING

W hat is meditation, anyway? You're probably thinking of someone sitting cross-legged on the floor (or "crisscross applesauce," as my child might say). Then this same person is loudly chanting OM for all to hear, with thumb and index finger touching in a mudra ...

Well meditation can certainly be that, if that's how one chooses to meditate. It can be also done sitting in a chair and lying down. Yes, I did say lying down. If you fall asleep, that's your body's way of telling you sleep may be a bit more important than this meditation stuff at the moment.

But before you figure out your ideal position, what is meditation for? Most likely you may have heard that meditation is about achieving inner peace, and quieting the mind, and that's correct.

There are other benefits to meditation. Meditation has been proven to have a significant therapeutic effect on both physical and mental conditions. Having trouble with anxiety? It can help decrease anxiety symptoms, increasing coping skills during times of high anxiety or stress. Difficulty with chronic or debilitating pain? Meditation can assist with that, stilling the mind, helping you control your responses to the pain, which in turn can lessen the pain's negative effect on you.

When done regularly, meditation can enhance self-awareness and promote personal and spiritual growth. In its more advanced forms, meditation can take you beyond a "self"-centered perspective of yourself and your immediate surroundings to an exploration of all that we are connected with.

Best of all, meditation can be done at your own pace, on your own time, in your own unique way. So starting off for a few minutes a day is better than nothing. Find a time and a place where you will not be disturbed, even if this means waiting until the kids are in bed or before they get up as you sip your coffee or tea in silence. At work and need to center yourself? Go outside, weather permitting, or into another room, or sit quietly in your own space for a few seconds, and don't forget to breathe.

Clearing the lungs of old stale air and letting fresh air reach down deep into your organs is very cleansing and refreshing. Here is a breathing technique you can try. You can do this by breathing in through your nose, counting slowly to four, holding your breath in for two counts, and then exhaling (through the nose or mouth, whichever you prefer) slowly to the count of four. This can be a great pick-me-up any time of day.

Meditation is something that helps center me, and it allows me to be more focused on what needs to be done that day. Of course I experience many other benefits as well. I personally use different techniques based on my needs at the time.

If you're finding it difficult to start a meditation practice, there are many good resources out there on the internet and even at the public library. Some of the benefits of guided imagery/meditation include:

- health and healing
- grounding
- relaxation
- pain relief

- stress relief
- stilling a restless mind
- decreasing anger
- decreasing anxiety
- releasing fear
- coping with grief
- increasing self-awareness
- forgiveness of self and others
- creating abundance
- increasing creativity
- connecting with Higher Self
- creating an inner sanctuary, a sacred space within (a place you can return to every time you meditate)
- increased amount and use of intuitive abilities
- connecting with Spirit Guides or Guardian Angels

The following is an example, and results vary with each individual and circumstance. One example is of guided imagery/meditation that I used with one of my clients. It was primarily focused on health and healing. The client experienced an unexplained mass on her breast. We utilized techniques to decrease her anxiety in regard to her health concern, and I used guided visualizations for the client to "picture" the mass reducing in size. The client has since visited her health care provider, who stated the mass no longer existed. This happened several years ago, and the last time we met she was still symptom-free.

Another great example of visualization is focused on grounding. Feeling flighty? Frequently bumping into things? Always seem to be rushing around and making choices without thinking them through? That may be a sign that you are ungrounded, meaning you are in your body but it's on autopilot because your consciousness is not fully in your body. Simply put, you are "out there"; detached. Many times this sense of detachment feels pleasant because things around you feel different or lighter. People may experience this after meditating or simply by going through the motions and detaching themselves from all that is around them. Pleasant experience or not, it may cause the above-mentioned results.

Most importantly, you want to be grounded to make the best decisions for yourself. You are here to have experiences, and some may not be pleasurable. However, detaching yourself from everything will keep you from experiencing the richness of the enjoyable experiences along with the not so enjoyable. Simply put, grounding is being in the present moment, fully aware of your surroundings, with a sense of calm and inner peace. This heightened level of conscious awareness that you are connected to all that is around you increases your ability to positively cope with difficult circumstances.

A few ways to become grounded include starting with the breathing technique discussed above. This can be used to slow everything down and get you focused on the present moment. This is where you focus on the here and now, releasing concerns about the past and worries about the future, as these keep you from truly experiencing the present moment. You can use this breathing technique along with the other techniques that follow. I personally have observed a remarkable decline in anxiety symptoms of clients as they used this technique.

Earthing is one technique used to become grounded. This is where you find a grassy area preferably free of debris and pesticides. Take off your shoes and socks and place your feet on the ground. Do this for at least five minutes at a time. Those who are clairsentient may be able to feel energy as it is either leaving through the bottom of his or her feet or as it is coming up through his or her feet. Even if you believe that you can't feel the energy, with practice this may open up your senses so that you start to feel the energy. Regardless if you feel the energy or not most likely you will feel better after Earthing as it naturally assists in clearing your energetic fields and grounding you. You can also connect with nature and ground by hiking, gardening, or simply taking a walk.

Focused thought assists with grounding. Allowing your thoughts to remain focused on what you are doing will help with grounding. Taking a walk? Observe the area around you. See the colors of the foliage. Smell the fragrant flowers. Listen to the sounds around you. Acknowledge random thoughts as they pop up in your mind about work, daily life, etc. Then let them float by like a cloud and continue what you are doing. Acknowledging your thoughts will actually help decrease their amount and intensity. What you resist persists. So becoming frustrated and trying to force the thoughts to stop may do the opposite.

Using stones for grounding. Crystal therapy is one of the healing modalities that I use; this includes using crystals and stones. Often times you may see both lumped under the term crystal. However there is a significant difference between both. Crystals cannot be used for grounding. I have had many conversations with individuals that have used high vibrational crystals without fully understanding them causing them to experience unpleasant side effects. Improper use might cause headaches, nausea, and other side effects such as the individual becoming ungrounded. There are some crystals that are toxic when handled, or their dust is breathed in.

Many purchase crystals for the metaphysical or spiritual properties that are listed for that specific crystal. "Why do people sell crystals without telling people that this can happen?" I am often asked this after assisting people to ground their energy after improper use of a crystal. Often times just like with any other product the seller is focused on the sell. Let's say you like to frequent a well-known fast food restaurant. When you go there do they tell you the possible downside to eating their meals especially in the long term? Of course not! On the other hand there are people that sell crystals and they do not have any idea of what can happen. They are just doing their job. As with anything else that you purchase it's up to you to make an informed decision. Crystals are excellent tools for healing especially when used by a healer that uses them with discretion and discernment.

If you choose to use stones for grounding the following work very well, black tourmaline, red jasper, agate, and hematite. Intuitively pick one and place it in your hand for a few minutes to see how you feel. If you feel ok or a slight heaviness (but not unpleasant) associated with that stone grounding your energy hold it or put it in your pocket for five minutes to start. Red jasper can be kept in your pocket for long periods of time. It is very useful as a "worry" bead, to be handled frequently as it calms emotions and grounds your energy simultaneously. Whichever stone or crystal you choose to use be aware of how you feel when using it. Listen to and honor your intuition. An easy way to cleanse a crystal or stone after each use is by picturing it surrounded by a white light. Focus with the intention of the light clearing away all lower vibrational energy that it picked up or absorbed.

Another technique would be to use the visualization as described below. You may wish to have someone read the following visualization to you, or you may want to read it and record it yourself with background music. As with any visualizations or meditations, they become easier with practice, and you may be able to remember them without a recording.

Sit in a quiet place, close your eyes, and start the breathing technique mentioned a few pages earlier. When you feel that your breathing is even and not labored, I want you to visualize yourself as a strong tree, such as a redwood, tall and majestic. As you breathe in, you are receiving energy and nutrients from the great central sun that shines down upon you.

Keep breathing as you feel the warmth of the sun penetrate you through the crown of your head and flow down throughout your body. As you continue to breathe, this energy flows, and each body part—your head, brain, brain stem, behind your eyes, in your jaw— is relaxing, releasing all tension stored there.

This energy continues down your neck, into your spinal cord, into your upper chest and back. Into your torso and lower back, this energy continues down into your hips and pelvic region. Relaxing, restoring, invigorating.

As this energy splits at the pelvic region and down each thigh, I want you to visualize great tree roots moving down your thighs. These roots are big and strong. They continue down your knees into your calves. These roots continue down your calves, into your feet, and out the bottom of your feet into the earth. These roots go deep down into Mother Earth, past great roots, rock beds, past her crystal caves, and into the great magma core, where you are grounded very deeply into the earth.

As you continue to breathe, you feel this grounding energy on all levels as Mother Earth supports you. You feel the energy pulsate throughout your body. It is a loving, nurturing, healing energy. You feel strong. You feel anchored. You feel secure.

As you slowly bring your awareness back into your body, gently move your fingers and toes, moving your wrists, feeling the temperature of the room around you.

I will count back to five, where you will open your eyes; you'll feel grounded, refreshed, and ready to continue your day. One, two ... becoming more aware; three ... hearing the sounds all around you. Four ... feeling your body temperature get acclimated to the room. Now five ... you are fully alert, well grounded in your body, connected to the earth and feeling wonderful.

Feel free to use this meditation daily or at any time that you may feel ungrounded. Doing a personal check-in on yourself daily, especially in the morning and throughout the day, will help assess where you are and help you get back to center more quickly each time you practice.

Wherever your path takes you meditation can be a great tool to go down that path with a clear mind, a greater sense of self, and clear intentions no matter what the future holds.

Closing

Your words have energy. Your thoughts and feelings are energy. Your words, actions, and deeds are energy. That energy can be perceived as positive or negative. How you choose to see yourself, others, and your life experiences is a choice. Be active in your life. Be the conductor, not the train. Ask yourself, "How can I change my present situation?" This can be as simple as seeing it how you would like to see it. Not something far away in the future but as you would like to see it now. Putting that energy powered by your new positive emotion toward the change will alter your life.

Each and every day, ask yourself, "What would I like to create today?" and "What can I do to create this?"

May you create with a higher purpose, and may your life be lived fully and balanced. And may you always remember that you are love and are loved.

With Many Blessings,
Tabby

NOTES

ABOUT THE AUTHOR

T abby graduated from The Ohio State University with a Masters Degree in Social Work with a concentration on Clinical Mental Health, and a Bachelor's of Social Work at Capital University. She also has Reiki Advanced Degrees in the Usui System of Natural Healing and a Certificate in Spirituality, Health & Healing. Honoring her spiritual abilities Tabby uses mental alchemy, and various energy/holistic therapy techniques to decode, transmute and heal the mind, body, emotions and spirit. Tabby lives in Ohio with her family and owns Oasis Of The Heart, LLC Wellness Center providing various traditional and holistic therapies. In addition, Tabby facilitates workshops and enjoys creating crystal jewelry and organic skin care, which she infuses with healing energy. You can visit her website at www.oasisoftheheart.com

Printed in the United States
By Bookmasters